Level E

PEARSON

AGS Globe

Shoreview, Minnesota

AMP™ QReads™ is based upon the instructional routine developed by **Elfrieda (Freddy) H. Hiebert** (Ph.D., University of Wisconsin—Madison). Professor Hiebert is Adjunct Professor at the University of California, Berkeley and has been a classroom teacher, university-based teacher, and educator for over 35 years. She has published over 130 research articles and chapters in journals and books on how instruction and materials influence reading acquisition. Professor Hiebert's TExT model for accessible texts has been used to develop widely-used reading programs, including *QuickReads®* and *QuickReads® Technology* (Pearson Learning Group).

The publisher wishes to thank the following educators for their helpful comments during the review process for *AMP™ QReads™*. Their assistance has been invaluable:

Shelley Al-Khatib, Teacher, Life Skills, Chippewa Middle School, North Oaks, MN; **Ann Ertl,** ESL Department Lead, Champlin Park High School, Champlin, MN; **Dr. Kathleen Sullivan,** Supervisor, Reading Services Center, Omaha Public Schools, Omaha, NE; **Ryan E. Summers,** Teacher, English, Neelsville Middle School, Germantown, MD.

Acknowledgments appear on page 176, which constitutes an extension of this copyright page.

ISBN-13: 978-0-7854-6306-1
ISBN-10: 0-7854-6306-2

1 2 3 4 5 6 7 8 9 10   11 10 09 08 07

1-800-992-0244
www.agsglobe.com

CONTENTS

Science

	Page	Audio Tracks

Arts and Culture

Social Studies

Literature and Language

Welcome to QReads™!

Please follow these steps for each page of readings:

FIRST READ

1. Read the Fast Facts and think about what you might already know about the topic. Look for two words that are new or difficult. Draw a line under these words.

2. Read the page aloud or silently to yourself. Always include the title at the top of the same page. Take as much time as you need.

3. Find the first page in Building Connections. Write some words or phrases there to help you remember what is important.

SECOND READ

1. Listen and read along silently with your teacher or the audio track.

2. Use the target rate of 1 minute when listening and reading along.

3. Ask yourself, what is one thing to remember? Answer the Key Notes question to help find what is important.

THIRD READ

1. Now, try to read as much of the page as you can within 1 minute.

2. Read silently as you are timed for 1 minute. Read aloud with a partner or your teacher. Circle the last word you read at the end of 1 minute.

3. Write down the number of words you read on the page. Review in your mind what is important to remember.

4. Complete the questions or other reading given by your teacher.

Eating for Energy

Good food choices give your body lots of energy.

Fast Facts

- One gram of carbohydrates provides about 4 calories.

- One gram of fat provides about 9 calories.

- Teens generally need 2,200 to 2,800 calories a day.

Healthful Eating

Food provides energy for everything you do, from using a computer to playing sports. Nutrition is the science that studies[22] how bodies use food. Everyone has different nutritional needs because everyone needs different amounts of energy.[38]

Food energy is measured in calories. One calorie is the amount of energy needed to raise the temperature of 1 gram of[60] water 1 degree. Fruits, vegetables, and grains are good sources of calories.[72]

You can create a nutritious diet by choosing and preparing your food wisely. Bananas provide better nutrition than candy.[91] That's because candy gives you quick energy, but that energy soon fades. Baked potatoes also provide better nutrition than fried potatoes. That's because fried potatoes add fat to your diet.[121]

KEY NOTES

Healthful Eating
What is healthful eating?

_____

_____

Eating for Energy

If a food group is near the top of the Food Pyramid, eat less of that food.

Fast Facts

- The revised Food Pyramid was introduced in 2005.

- Fifteen percent of Americans 12 to 19 years old are overweight.

- Foods with sugar often have "empty calories," making you feel full but providing few nutrients.

The Food Pyramid

People who study how bodies use food are called nutritionists. Nutritionists divide food into five main groups. A healthful diet has a balance of foods from all five groups.[32]

The five food groups are grains, vegetables, fruits, dairy products, and meat and beans. Your body also needs fats, but only in small amounts.[56]

The Food Pyramid shows what kinds of foods make up a balanced diet. Using the pyramid helps you choose the right[77] amounts of food from each group and reminds you that exercise is also important for health.[93]

A healthful diet helps keep you fit. It gives you the energy you need to perform well in school and in sports, and it helps you enjoy spending time with friends.[124]

KEY NOTES

The Food Pyramid
What is the Food Pyramid?

_____

_____

Nutrition Facts

Serving Size 1 Tbsp (14g)
Servings Per Container 32

Amount Per Serving

Calories 100   Calories from Fat 100

% Daily Value*

Total Fat 11g	**17%**
Saturated Fat 7g	**36%**
Cholesterol 30mg	**10%**
Sodium 90mg	**4%**
Total Carbohydrate 0g	**0%**
Protein 0g	

Vitamin A 8%

Not a significant source of dietary fiber, sugars, vitamin C, calcium and iron.

*Percent Daily Values are based on a 2,000 calorie diet.

INGREDIENTS: CREAM, SALT, ANNATTO (FOR COLOR)

SWEET CREAM • SALT

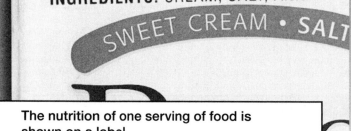

The nutrition of one serving of food is shown on a label.

Fast Facts

- The Nutrition Labeling and Education Act was passed in 1990.

- Nutrition label percentages are based on 2,000 calories a day.

- Nutrition label information is based on *one serving* of a food in a package, not on *all* the food in the package.

Nutrition Labels

Nutrition labels tell us if a food meets our nutritional needs. They list the amounts of nutrients that are in one serving of a [26] food, including carbohydrates and fats. Nutrition labels also list how much of each nutrient you need every day. This number is [47] listed as a percent of the total number of calories many people eat in a day. [63]

Nutrition labels can help you choose healthful foods. They can show you that eating pasta is a better choice than eating [84] potato chips. That's because pasta's carbohydrates give you energy that lasts longer. [96]

The next time you buy food, even a snack, read the nutrition label. It can help you choose a food that can keep you healthy and strong. [123]

KEY NOTES
Nutrition Labels
What do nutrition labels show?
_____
_____

Eating for Energy

Fruits and vegetables contain Vitamin C.

Fast Facts

- There are 13 vitamins: A, C, D, E, K, and 8 vitamins called the B complex.

- One way you can get vitamin D is from sunlight.

- You need some minerals in very small amounts. These minerals are called trace elements.

Vitamins and Minerals

Two kinds of nutrients you get from food are vitamins and minerals. Vitamins help your body change food into energy[23] and build strength. Vitamin A is needed for healthy skin and strong bones. Vitamin B12 helps your body form new red blood cells. Vitamin C is important for good teeth and helps fight colds.[57]

Minerals help you grow and stay healthy. They build strong bones and teeth and keep your muscles and nerves healthy. Iron[78] is a mineral that helps oxygen get to your red blood cells. The mineral copper helps your body use iron.[98]

Your body works hard all day. You can keep it working well by eating right to get the vitamins and minerals you need.[121]

KEY NOTES

Vitamins and Minerals

What are vitamins and minerals?

_____

_____

Eating for Energy

Healthful Eating

1. Why does your body need food?

    a. Food provides energy for everything you do.
    b. Food is a good source of energy.
    c. Food helps you use a computer and play sports.
    d. all of the above

2. How can you create a nutritious diet?

    a. by choosing foods that taste good
    b. by eating only fruits and vegetables
    c. by choosing and preparing food wisely
    d. by eating foods that have lots of energy

3. Why should different people eat different amounts of food?

_____

_____

_____

The Food Pyramid

1. What does the Food Pyramid show?

    a. the kinds of foods you can buy in stores
    b. the kinds of foods that are in a balanced diet
    c. the kinds of fruits and vegetables you should eat
    d. the kinds of foods that nutritionists like to eat

2. What else does the Food Pyramid show?

_____

_____

_____

3. What are some benefits of a healthful diet?

_____

_____

_____

Nutrition Labels

1. Nutrition labels show _____

    a. how the food is prepared.
    b. the amount of energy in the nutrients.
    c. how much one serving of a food costs.
    d. the nutrients in one serving of a food.

2. Nutrition labels are meant to help people _____

    a. know how a food tastes.
    b. prepare a food.
    c. balance their diet.
    d. know who made the food.

3. Why should people read nutrition labels before they buy or eat food?

_____

_____

_____

Vitamins and Minerals

1. Why do you need vitamins and minerals?

    a. to build strength
    b. to stay healthy
    c. to help your body work well
    d. all of the above

2. What are two ways your body uses vitamins?

_____

_____

_____

3. What are two ways your body uses minerals?

_____

_____

_____

nutrition	calorie	nutritionists	pyramid
carbohydrates	nutrients	vitamin	mineral

1. Choose the word from the word box above that best matches each definition. Write the word on the line below.

A. _____ people who study food and how bodies use it

B. _____ things found in foods that provide nutrition

C. _____ nutrients that are found in pasta and other grains

D. _____ a kind of nutrient that helps your body build healthy skin and teeth

E. _____ a kind of nutrient that helps your body get oxygen to your blood cells

F. _____ a unit that is used to measure the energy in food

G. _____ the science that studies how the body uses food

H. _____ a shape with a point at the top and a broad base

2. Fill in the blanks in the sentences below. Choose the word from the word box that completes each sentence.

A. To check his diet, Marco listed the _____ in all of the foods he ate.

B. Alex went to school to study _____ because he was interested in foods.

C. Sara watched the _____ counts of the foods she ate so she could lose weight.

D. The Food _____ tells you how to balance your diet.

E. Iron is a kind of _____ that helps our red blood cells get oxygen.

F. There is a lot of _____ C in oranges and other fruits.

G. Karen talked to several _____ to make sure she ate properly before the race.

H. Bread has a rich supply of _____.

Eating for Energy

1. Use the chart to help you remember what you read. In the right column, complete the sentences that begin in the left column.

A. To eat right for energy, we should _____	
B. The Food Pyramid helps us to _____	
C. Nutrition labels help us to _____	
D. Vitamins help our bodies _____	
E. Minerals help our bodies _____	

2. Why is it important to eat healthfully?

_____

_____

_____

_____

3. What would you tell someone who wanted to learn to eat healthfully?

_____

_____

_____

_____

4. What are two changes you can make to your diet so you will eat more healthfully?

_____

_____

_____

_____

Earth's Moon

A full moon rises behind a mountain.

Fast Facts

- The Moon is about 2,160 miles across.

- The Moon is one-quarter the size of Earth.

- If Earth were the size of a basketball, the Moon would be the size of a tennis ball.

Earth's Satellite

Of the many bodies in our solar system, the Moon is the closest to Earth. It is almost 239,000 miles from our planet.[25] On Earth, that distance is considered far away. However, in space it is considered extremely close.[41]

The Moon appears in the night sky because it is a satellite of Earth. A satellite is a body that orbits a larger body. As Earth's[67] satellite, the Moon orbits Earth. It also travels with Earth as our planet orbits the Sun.[83]

While it travels with Earth, the Moon turns. Earth turns, too. Because both Earth and the Moon are always turning, one side[105] of the Moon is never seen from Earth. This side is called the far side of the Moon.[123]

KEY NOTES

Earth's Satellite
What is a satellite?

_____

_____

Earth's Moon

The moon's gravity causes the ocean tides to rise and fall.

Fast Facts

- Ancient Greeks and Romans thought tides were caused by Earth breathing.

- Modern ideas about tides started in 1687.

- Each day, tides occur 50 minutes later than the day before.

The Moon and Tides

If you've been to the ocean, you know that the water level at the beach changes during the day. At low tide, you see more sand. At high tide, you see more water.[37]

Tides on Earth are largely caused by the Moon. The Moon's gravity pulls slightly on the oceans, causing the oceans to rise.[59] In this way, the force of the Moon's gravity causes the rising and falling of tides.[75]

The height of the tides is affected by the shape of the coastline and the depth of the ocean. The highest tides on[98] Earth occur in a bay in eastern Canada. During high tide, the height of the water in this bay increases by as much as 53 feet.[124]

KEY NOTES

The Moon and Tides
What is the difference between high and low tide?

_____

_____

Earth's Moon

From Earth, we see four phases of the Moon.

Fast Facts

- The Moon moves through space at about 2,300 miles per hour.

- The Moon's orbit around Earth is about 1.4 million miles.

- The Moon is kept in orbit around Earth by the pull of Earth's gravity.

The Changing Moon

Although the Moon seems to give off light, its light really comes from the Sun. The Moon also seems to change size, but what really changes is how much of the Moon we see.[37]

The Moon orbits Earth about every 29 days. During this time, the Moon goes through several lunar phases. The first[57] lunar phase is called a new moon. At this time, we see only a small part of the Moon. Over the next two weeks, more of the[84] Moon becomes visible until we see an entire side of the Moon. This phase is called full moon. Over the next two weeks, less[108] of the Moon becomes visible until there's another new moon. Then, a new lunar phase begins.[124]

KEY NOTES

The Changing Moon
What do we see during a full moon?

_____

_____

Earth's Moon

In 1969, an astronaut walked on the Moon for the first time.

Fast Facts

- During the day, the Moon's rocks are about the temperature of boiling water.

- At night, the Moon is colder than any place on Earth.

- On the Moon, the sky is always black and the stars can always be seen.

Humans on the Moon

From 1969 to 1972, twelve American astronauts flew missions to the Moon. Before taking off, the astronauts had to carefully prepare for these missions. [28]

Because the Moon does not have oxygen, food, or water, astronauts have to carry these things so they can survive. [48] Astronauts also have to learn how to walk on the Moon because the Moon's gravity is only one-sixth that of Earth. This lower [72] gravity makes people weigh less, so they bounce when they try to walk on the Moon. [88]

When the Space Age began, some people were afraid that one country might try to rule space. Today, however, people [108] from many countries fly missions together so that everyone can study the Moon and space. [123]

KEY NOTES

Humans on the Moon

How easy would it be to live on the Moon?

_____

_____

Earth's Moon

Earth's Satellite

1. Around what two bodies does the Moon orbit?

  a. the Sun and a star
  b. Earth and the Sun
  c. a satellite and a planet
  d. Earth and the solar system

2. Which of the following is a fact about the Moon?

  a. Earth travels around the Moon.
  b. The Moon is a satellite of Earth.
  c. All sides of the Moon can be seen from Earth.
  d. The Moon is not part of the solar system.

3. Why do you think 239,000 miles is considered "extremely close" in space?

  _____

  _____

  _____

The Moon and Tides

1. Tides are largely caused by _____

  a. the Sun's gravity pulling on the Moon.
  b. the Moon's gravity pulling on Earth's oceans.
  c. the force of ocean water washing over sand.
  d. the force of Earth's gravity on the Atlantic Ocean.

2. What is the difference between high tide and low tide?

_____

_____

_____

3. What two things do the height of the tides depend on?

_____

_____

_____

The Changing Moon

1. The light we see from the Moon _____

    a. comes from the Sun.
    b. comes from Earth.
    c. comes from other planets.
    d. comes from other moons.

2. Why does the Moon's size seem to change over a month?

    a. The amount of the Moon that is visible from Earth changes.
    b. The Moon's size decreases as it moves away from Earth.
    c. The Moon is always visible when the lunar phases start.
    d. The moon's size increases as it moves toward the Sun.

3. What are the lunar phases?

_____

_____

_____

Humans on the Moon

1. The main idea of "Humans on the Moon" is _____

    a. how astronauts were chosen to go to the Moon.
    b. how astronauts learned to walk on the Moon.
    c. how astronauts found oxygen and water on the Moon.
    d. the problems astronauts face on the Moon.

2. When astronauts go to the Moon, why do they have to carry everything they need to survive?

_____

_____

_____

3. Why do humans have to learn how to walk on the Moon?

_____

_____

_____

astronauts	orbits	gravity	phases
lunar	satellite	missions	tide

1. Choose the word from the word box above that best matches each definition. Write the word on the line below.

A. _____ special tasks given to a person or a group

B. _____ the regular rising and falling of a body of water

C. _____ the force that pulls planets or moons toward each other

D. _____ paths taken by bodies in the solar system as they go around other bodies

E. _____ people who travel into space

F. _____ a body in the solar system that travels around another body

G. _____ stages in a cycle of events

H. _____ having to do with the Moon

2. Fill in the blank in the sentences below. Choose the word from the word box that completes each sentence.

A. To see when the Moon would be full, Jill looked at a _____ calendar.

B. Since the 1960s, there have been many _____ to explore space.

C. The Moon is a _____ of Earth.

D. The Moon goes through different _____ as it circles Earth.

E. The rise and fall of Earth's oceans is largely caused by the pull of the Moon's _____.

F. We left the beach just as the _____ was rising.

G. In 1969, American _____ became the first people to land on the Moon.

H. The Moon _____ Earth as Earth travels through space.

Earth's Moon

1. Use the chart to help you remember what you read. Write the main idea and one important detail from each passage.

Earth's Satellite	
Main Idea:	Detail:

The Moon and Tides	
Main Idea:	Detail:

The Changing Moon	
Main Idea:	Detail:

Humans on the Moon	
Main Idea:	Detail:

2. Write three things you have learned about Earth's Moon in this topic.

_____

_____

_____

_____

3. What are two things that astronauts might learn from visiting the Moon?

_____

_____

_____

_____

4. Do you think you might like to go to the Moon? Why or why not?

_____

_____

_____

_____

Heat and Energy

Riding a bike can generate heat in your body.

Fast Facts

- Scientists once believed that heat was an invisible liquid.

- The idea that heat is a form of energy was proved in the 1800s.

- Friction can damage machines. Oil is used in machines to reduce friction.

Generating Heat

When your hands feel cold, you rub them together to warm them. The faster you rub your hands, the warmer they[23] feel. Rubbing your hands together moves the particles in your hands. The faster you rub your hands, the faster the particles[44] move. As the particles move against one another, they create a force called friction. This friction creates heat.[62]

Whenever there is heat, energy is being generated. When you rub your hands together, walk, run, ride a bicycle, or climb[83] stairs, your body changes the food you eat into energy. The heat that you feel in your body after doing these activities comes from[107] the energy your body has generated. Your body generates and uses energy all the time.[122]

KEY NOTES

Generating Heat
How does rubbing your hands together make them warm?

_____

_____

Heat and Energy

The liquid inside a thermometer goes down as the temperature drops.

Temperature

Temperature is a measure of how hot or cold something is. Tools that measure temperature are called thermometers.[19] Thermometers can measure the temperature of our bodies, the air, and food.[31]

Some thermometers have a thin tube with liquid inside. When the temperature around the thermometer gets warmer,[48] the liquid expands and rises in the tube. That's because heat causes the molecules, or small parts of the liquid, to move[70] farther apart. When the temperature gets colder, the liquid moves down in the tube. That's because cooler temperatures[88] cause the molecules in the liquid to contract, or move closer together.[100]

Marks on a thermometer show the temperature in degrees on a scale. The degree at which the liquid stops shows the temperature.[122]

KEY NOTES

Temperature
What is a thermometer?

_____

_____

Heat and Energy

Wearing white clothing in hot weather can help you feel cooler.

Fast Facts

- Some ancient Greeks thought people saw color because rays shot from their eyes.

- Light is made up of waves. We see different light waves as different colors.

- Some scientists believe that people can see up to 10 million colors.

Colors and Heat

People who live in hot climates often wear white or light-colored clothes. People who live in cold climates often wear[24] black or dark-colored clothes. This is because white clothes make you feel cooler, while black clothes make you feel warmer.[45]

White and black materials work with light in different ways. Light bounces off white material. Because white clothes do not[65] absorb light, you feel cooler when you wear white in hot weather. In contrast, black clothes absorb light. When the[85] particles in the material absorb light, they move around. As the particles move against one another, they create friction and the[106] material heats up. That's why you feel hotter when you wear black on a hot day.[122]

KEY NOTES

Colors and Heat   Underline the most important sentence in the passage. Explain your choice.

_____

_____

Heat and Energy

Insulation inside the walls keeps buildings
cool in summer and warm in winter.

Fast Facts

- Plastic and wooden pot
  handles don't conduct heat,
  so they usually stay cool
  enough to touch.

- Wearing layers of clothing
  helps your body trap heat
  in several places.

- The air between two windows
  doesn't move, so it doesn't
  conduct heat.

How Heat Moves

It's cold outside. To stay warm, you put on boots, a heavy coat, a hat, and gloves. Your clothes become insulators against [25] the cold. Insulators trap your body heat and keep the cold air away from you. Insulators keep homes warm, too. Home [46] insulation keeps the cold air outside in winter and the hot air outside in summer. [61]

Material that lets heat move from place to place is called a conductor. Metal can be a good conductor. If you put a metal [85] spoon in warm water, the metal conducts the heat in the water to the spoon, which gets warm. A wooden spoon does not [108] conduct as much heat. That's why it's safer to stir something warm with a wooden spoon. [124]

KEY NOTES

How Heat Moves
How does a coat keep you warm?

_____

_____

Heat and Energy

Generating Heat

1. "Generating Heat" is MAINLY about _____

    a. changing food into friction.
    b. particles that make heat.
    c. how people make and use energy.
    d. why friction is generated.

2. Whenever there is heat, _____

    a. energy is created.
    b. there is danger.
    c. energy is wasted.
    d. there is food.

3. Why do you feel hot when you walk or ride your bike?

_____

_____

_____

Temperature

1. What is temperature?

    a. a measure that contracts and expands
    b. something that shows when it will snow or rain
    c. a measure of how hot or cold something is
    d. a warning that something is about to happen

2. Why does the liquid in a thermometer expand when the temperature is warm?

_____

_____

_____

3. Why does the liquid in a thermometer move down the tube when the temperature is cold?

_____

_____

_____

Colors and Heat

1. The main idea of "Colors and Heat" is that _____

    a. light bounces off black clothing.
    b. light in hot climates is hotter than light in other places.
    c. light is absorbed by white clothing in winter.
    d. light acts differently on black materials than on white materials.

2. Black clothes make you feel hot because _____

    a. black material absorbs light.
    b. light bounces off dark material.
    c. black material is often worn in cool climates.
    d. light can remove color from dark material.

3. On a hot summer day, what type of clothing can make you feel cooler? Why?

_____

_____

_____

How Heat Moves

1. Which of the following best describes how an insulator works?

    a. An insulator keeps heat from moving.
    b. Heat moves through an insulator.
    c. An insulator attracts heat.
    d. Heat is spread out by an insulator.

2. What is the difference between insulators and conductors?

_____

_____

_____

3. Why will a metal spoon get warm if you put it in a glass of warm water?

_____

_____

_____

absorb	friction	climates	generated
conductor	insulator	molecules	thermometers

1. Choose the word from the word box above that best matches each definition. Write the word on the line below.

A. _____ caused or created

B. _____ tools that measure temperature

C. _____ a material or object that keeps heat from moving from place to place

D. _____ to take something in

E. _____ a material or object that lets heat move from place to place

F. _____ very small parts of something

G. _____ the weather in different places

H. _____ the force created when particles rub against one another

2. Fill in the blanks in the sentences below. Choose the word from the word box that completes each sentence.

A. My new hat was a good _____ that helped me stay warm in the snow.

B. People used to make fire by rubbing sticks together to cause _____.

C. Doctors and nurses use _____ to see if people have fevers.

D. The _____ in the liquid move apart as the liquid's temperature rises.

E. People who live in warmer _____ often wear white clothing to stay cool.

F. Eric _____ enough heat to stay warm when he ran home.

G. A wooden spoon is not a good _____ of heat, so it stays cool.

H. A dark shirt makes you feel warmer on a cool day because it will _____ light.

47

Heat and Energy

1. Complete each sentence below to help you remember what you read.

A. When particles move against one another,

_____

_____

B. Liquid in a thermometer rises in a tube

_____

_____

C. Liquid in a thermometer moves down in a tube

_____

_____

D. Wearing white pants in hot weather

_____

_____

E. Wearing a black shirt on a hot day

_____

_____

F. Insulation affects temperature by

_____

_____

G. Conductors affect temperature by

_____

_____

2. What are two ways to get warm that were described in these passages?

_____

_____

_____

_____

3. The liquid in a thermometer is going down. Describe why this is happening.

_____

_____

_____

_____

4. What would be the best thing to use to stir a hot liquid? Why?

_____

_____

_____

_____

Guitars

Instruments like guitars were played in ancient Egypt.

Fast Facts

- Early guitars had strings that were made from parts of animals.

- Plastic guitar strings were introduced in 1946.

- The smallest guitar was one-twentieth the thickness of a human hair.

Guitars Past and Present

A guitar is a stringed instrument. To make music on a guitar, people stroke or pick the strings. This movement makes the[26] strings vibrate. When the strings vibrate, they make sounds that create music.[38]

Most guitars have six strings. Some have four strings and others have as many as twelve. While many guitars are made of[60] wood, guitar strings are usually made of bronze, steel, or a special kind of plastic.[75]

Instruments like guitars were first made in ancient Egypt. Later, in the 700s, people from Africa invaded Spain. The[94] invaders brought with them an early type of guitar. From Spain, guitars were taken to other European countries. Over the next[115] several hundred years, people created different types of guitars. Today, guitars are played in countries around the world.[133]

KEY NOTES

Guitars Past and Present
How are guitars different from one another?

_____

_____

Guitars

Andres Segovia played a Spanish guitar with six strings.

Fast Facts

- Early Spanish guitars usually had sets of double strings.

- Antonio de Torres Jurado, the designer of the modern Spanish guitar, was also a carpenter.

- Some modern guitars have twelve strings, which make a deep, rich sound.

Spanish Guitars

Early guitars looked different from today's guitars. They were not as wide as modern guitars and they had a different [22] number of strings. In the late 1800s, a Spanish guitar maker changed the instrument's shape. His guitars looked more like the ones we play today. [47]

Guitars became very popular in Spain, where a special style of guitar music was developed. However, some musicians didn't [66] respect the instrument because composers of classical music did not write music for the guitar. They thought it couldn't be used to play classical music. [91]

A Spanish musician changed people's ideas about the guitar. He played classical music that had never before been played on [111] the guitar. He also wrote his own music for the guitar. Today, the guitar is one of the most popular musical instruments. [133]

KEY NOTES
Spanish Guitars   How did one musician change the way people thought about guitars?
_____
_____

Guitars

Electric guitars can make loud sounds.

Fast Facts

- Electric guitars use magnets to create electrical energy and sound.

- The first electric guitar became available to the public in the 1930s.

- One early electric guitar was called the Frying Pan because of its shape.

Acoustic and Electric Guitars

When a guitar string vibrates, it causes the soundboard, a wooden piece on the front of the guitar, to vibrate and make[26] sounds louder. Because the body of the guitar is hollow, it amplifies the vibration of the soundboard, making the sounds[46] of the strings louder and easier to hear. A guitar that makes sound in this way is called an acoustic guitar.[67]

An electric guitar makes sound in a different way. Most electric guitars are not hollow and do not have a soundboard to[89] amplify the strings' vibrations. Instead, they use an electronic signal to amplify the vibrations. This signal is sent to a speaker,[110] which can make the sound very loud. That's why music that's made on electric guitars is louder than music from acoustic guitars.[132]

KEY NOTES

Acoustic and Electric Guitars
How does an acoustic guitar make sound?

_____

_____

Guitars

Guitars have been used in rock music for many years.

Fast Facts

- Rock-and-roll music was created in the United States.

- In a rock band called the Beatles, three of the four musicians played guitars.

- The first big rock hit was "Rock Around the Clock" (1954).

Rock-and-Roll Music

In the 1950s, a new kind of music, called rock and roll, appeared. Teenagers enjoyed rock and roll because of its loud [26] music and fast beat, or rhythm. Compared to other kinds of music at that time, teenagers thought rock and roll was very [48] exciting, and they enjoyed dancing to its beat. The rhythms of the music often seemed more important than the words in the songs. [71]

Many of the musicians who first made rock and roll popular were guitar players. Most of them played electric guitars, which [92] became the most important instrument in rock music. Most of the bands people listen to probably have at least one guitar to [114] keep the music's rhythm. Rock music has changed over the years, but the guitar remains a big part of it. [134]

KEY NOTES

Rock-and-Roll Music
How are guitars used in rock music?

_____

_____

Guitars

Guitars Past and Present

1. How does a guitar make sound?

    a. the electricity makes the sound
    b. the wood vibrates
    c. the strings vibrate
    d. the strings hit the guitar

2. What does *vibration* mean?

    a. hitting something hard
    b. making music
    c. being afraid of something
    d. going back and forth quickly

3. Why do you think people created different kinds of guitars?

_____

_____

_____

Spanish Guitars

1. One difference between early guitars and today's guitars is _____

    a. early guitars were louder than modern guitars.
    b. early guitars had a different number of strings.
    c. modern guitars are much smaller.
    d. modern guitars are not as popular.

2. What important changes to the guitar took place in Spain?

_____

_____

_____

3. Why did people's opinion of the guitar change?

_____

_____

_____

Acoustic and Electric Guitars

1. An acoustic guitar _____

    a. uses an electronic signal to make its sound louder.

    b. does not use an electronic signal to make its sound louder.

    c. must be played with another instrument so it can be heard.

    d. has fewer strings than an electric guitar.

2. An electric guitar makes sound by _____

    a. using an electronic signal to make its sound louder.

    b. not using an electronic signal to make its sound louder.

    c. playing with an acoustic guitar.

    d. making fewer types of sounds than an acoustic guitar.

3. What kind of music do you think is best played on acoustic guitars? What kind is best played on electric guitars? Why?

_____

_____

_____

Rock-and-Roll Music

1. What is rhythm in music?

a. how popular it is
b. the loudness of the music
c. the beat of the music
d. the number of guitars in the band

2. Why did teenagers like rock music when it first appeared?

_____

_____

_____

3. Why do you think rock music is still popular today?

_____

_____

_____

acoustic	guitar	amplify	musicians
classical	teenagers	rhythm	vibrate

1. Choose the word from the word box above that best matches each definition. Write the word on the line below.

A. _____ an instrument that makes music with strings

B. _____ to shake or move from side to side

C. _____ the pattern of beats in music

D. _____ people who make music

E. _____ a musical instrument whose sound is not changed electronically

F. _____ people who are 13–19 years of age

G. _____ to make something louder

H. _____ relating to a type of music that has been made for many years

2. Fill in the blanks in the sentences below. Choose the word from the word box that completes each sentence.

A. An electronic signal can _____ the sound of a string.

B. _____ music is very different from rock music.

C. Picking a string makes it _____.

D. Some people prefer the _____ guitar to the electric guitar.

E. Some parents don't like the music that their _____ listen to.

F. The _____ in the band played all types of music.

G. Jack learned to play the _____ when he was twelve years old.

H. Maria loved the music's fast _____ because she could dance to it.

Guitars

1. Use the timeline to help you remember what you read. Arrange the following events in the order in which they occurred.

   • Rock music was introduced.

   • A Spanish guitar maker changed the shape of guitars.

   • The electric guitar was introduced.

   • The guitar was taken to other European countries.

   • The guitar was taken to Spain from Africa.

   • A Spanish musician showed that classical music could be played on the guitar.

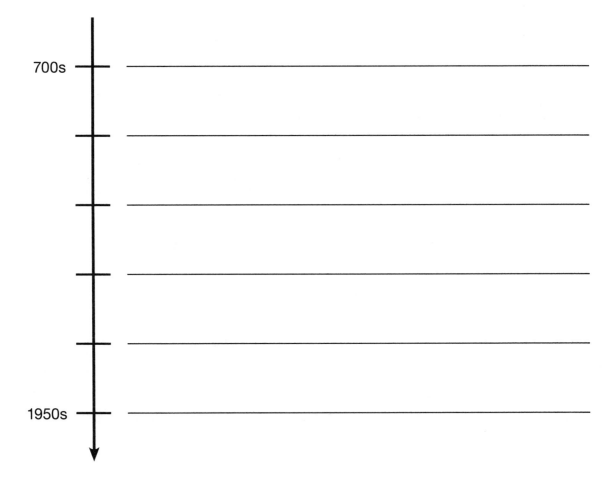

700s

1950s

2. List three facts you learned about guitars in these passages.

_____

_____

_____

_____

3. Why do you think guitars are so popular today?

_____

_____

_____

_____

4. Suppose there was another passage in this topic. Would you expect it to be about drums or about different kinds of guitar strings? Explain.

_____

_____

_____

_____

People in Pictures

This portrait shows a woman's profile.

Fast Facts

- Rembrandt, the Dutch painter, created nearly 80 self-portraits.

- Long ago, people wore miniature portraits inside pieces of jewelry.

- One of the most famous portraits is the *Mona Lisa*.

What Is a Portrait?

A portrait is a picture of a person. Portraits might be drawings, paintings, or photos. They might show an entire[24] person or just a face. The person in a portrait is called the subject. Some portraits show their subjects as they really look.[47] In others, subjects look the way the person who did the portrait sees them.[61]

Viewers can learn something about the subjects of portraits besides how they look. Some portraits show the subjects'[79] interests or work. For example, we can tell that a person who is wearing a military uniform served in the armed forces.[101]

Portraits can show a subject from the front or side. A side view is called a profile. Sometimes an artist does a portrait of himself or herself, which is called a self-portrait.[134]

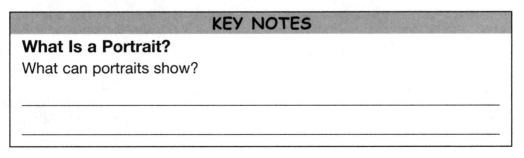

KEY NOTES

What Is a Portrait?
What can portraits show?

_____

_____

People in Pictures

This is a portrait of a family.

Fast Facts

- In ancient Egypt, portraits were painted on mummies.

- In England long ago, some people had tiny portrait paintings, called miniatures, which they wore as jewelry.

- A modern portrait painter named Chuck Close has painted huge portraits that are the size of billboards.

Paintings

Hundreds of years ago, most portraits were paintings. People who wanted pictures of themselves hired an artist to[19] paint their portrait. Because most people could not afford to do this, many portraits were pictures of people who were rich or[41] famous. These paintings were often realistic. That means the artist showed people as they really looked.[57]

Some portraits show groups of people, such as a married couple or a family. Group portraits provide extra information[76] because we learn about the important people in the subject's life.[87]

When we look at realistic paintings, we get an idea about what life was like in the time and place the person lived. For[111] example, the clothing a person is wearing in a portrait tells us what people wore at the time the portrait was painted.[133]

KEY NOTES

Paintings
What are realistic paintings?

_____

_____

People in Pictures

This portrait of Harriet Tubman was taken during the days of early photography.

Fast Facts

- The first photograph was taken in 1826.

- *Photograph* comes from two Greek words that mean "light" and "to write."

- Mathew Brady was a photographer who took thousands of photographs during the U.S. Civil War.

Photographs

In the 1800s, a new invention made it easier to create portraits. That invention was the camera. It was faster and easier to take a photograph than it was to paint a picture.[34]

The first photographs were in black and white. Photographers didn't have to decide what colors to use or[52] how to paint someone's face. However, they did decide on the background or what things would be in the photograph. In this[74] way, photographers helped determine what information people learned about the photograph's subject.[86]

At the time of the U.S. Civil War, the camera was still a new invention. One early photographer became famous by taking[108] pictures of soldiers. His work helped make photography more common and more popular. Today, photography is one of the main ways portraits are created.[132]

KEY NOTES

Photographs

How do photographers help people learn about their subjects?

_____

_____

People in Pictures

A caricature artist works on a drawing.

Fast Facts

- *Caricature* comes from an Italian word that means "exaggerate."

- The first important caricatures were created in Europe in the 1500s.

- One French artist was jailed for his caricature of the king.

Caricatures

One kind of portrait is called a caricature. A caricature uses exaggeration to tell us about a person. The artist takes[22] something about the person that stands out and makes it stand out even more. For example, if someone has a tiny nose, huge[45] ears, a large jaw, unusual eyes, or a certain kind of hair, the artist may exaggerate that part of the person. This is usually[69] done with humor. Sometimes artists exaggerate the way people act as well as how they look.[85]

Famous people are often the subjects of caricatures. You may have seen caricatures of world leaders or people in show[105] business. Newspapers often have caricatures of famous people that are drawn so well that you know who the person is as soon as you look at the picture.[133]

KEY NOTES

Caricatures
What is a caricature?

_____

_____

People in Pictures

What Is a Portrait?

1. Another good name for "What Is a Portrait?" is _____

    a. "Pictures of People."
    b. "Front Views and Side Views."
    c. "What Is a Subject?"
    d. "Self-Portraits."

2. Why did the author write "What Is a Portrait?"

    a. to compare front views and profiles
    b. to give readers information about portraits
    c. to tell about a famous portrait
    d. to explain what a self-portrait is

3. What is a portrait?

_____

_____

_____

Paintings

1. In this passage, *realistic* means _____

    a. something that is made up.
    b. a book that tells things that really happened.
    c. showing something as it really is.
    d. showing someone as the person wants to look.

2. Why are many portraits painted of people who were rich?

_____

_____

_____

3. Name three things we can learn about a person in a realistic painting.

_____

_____

_____

Photographs

1. Why did the camera make it easier to create portraits?

    a. The photographs were made in black and white.

    b. People could learn more about the subjects of the portraits.

    c. Taking photographs was faster and easier than painting.

    d. More people could fit in photographs.

2. Another good name for this passage is _____

    a. "Early Photographs."

    b. "How the Camera Was Invented."

    c. "How Photography Changed Making Portraits."

    d. "The Camera in the Civil War."

3. Name three ways photography changed the way that portraits are done.

_____

_____

_____

Caricatures

1. In this passage, what does _exaggeration_ mean?

_____

_____

_____

2. Another good name for this passage is _____

    a. "Caricatures Have Funny Faces."
    b. "A Special Kind of Portrait."
    c. "Portraits in the News."
    d. "Tiny Noses and Big Ears."

3. Explain your choice in question 2.

_____

_____

_____

portrait	artist	photograph	invention
caricature	realistic	subject	exaggerate

1. Choose the word from the word box above that best matches each definition. Write the word on the line below.

A. _____ a picture taken with a camera

B. _____ a picture of a person

C. _____ something that looks as it really is

D. _____ to make something stand out

E. _____ something that is created

F. _____ a person who makes art

G. _____ a person in a portrait

H. _____ a portrait that exaggerates a person's looks or actions

2. Fill in the blanks in the sentences below. Choose the word from the word box that completes each sentence.

A. I took a _____ of the new baby.

B. Martin watched the _____ paint a painting.

C. We could tell that the _____ of the painting was a rich man.

D. The _____ changed the way portraits were done.

E. I was happy to pose for a _____.

F. The caricature didn't _____ the size of the woman's eyes.

G. The painting was very _____, so we recognized Anita.

H. The _____ of the teacher made the class laugh.

People in Pictures

1. Use the idea web to help you remember what you read. In each box, write the main idea of the passage.

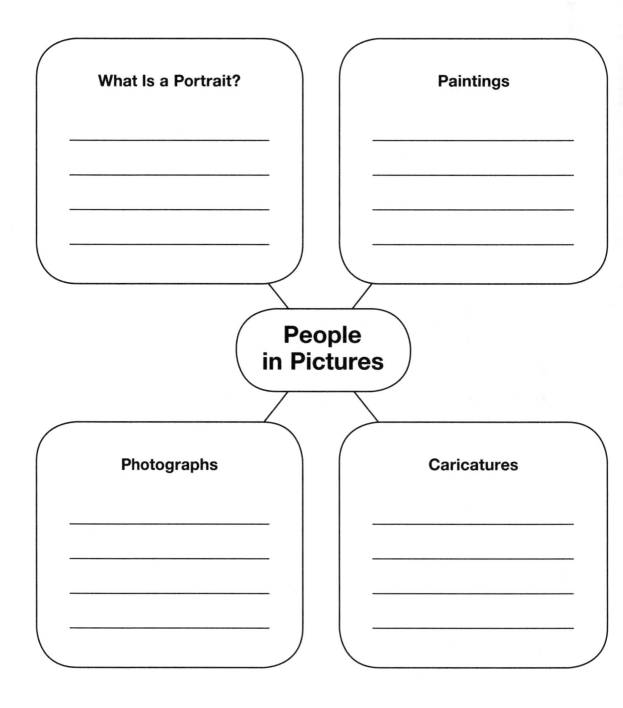

What Is a Portrait?

Paintings

People in Pictures

Photographs

Caricatures

2. What can you learn about a person from a portrait?

_____

_____

_____

_____

3. Why do you think there are so many ways to have a portrait done?

_____

_____

_____

_____

4. If you could have a portrait done of yourself, what kind of portrait would you choose? Explain.

_____

_____

_____

_____

Music in the Movies

Early movies had no sound, but music was played during the movie.

Fast Facts

- The music part of a film is called the score.

- Early films were silent. They did not have sound.

- The first "talking" movie in the United States was made in 1927.

Music in the Movies

When you watch a movie, you're also listening to it. You're listening to the words the characters speak and to the movie's [26] music. Sometimes you're not fully aware of the music. The director may use music to help set a scene or to help tell the story that is taking place. [55]

At other times, the director wants you to be aware of the music. Certain music might be used to represent a character. [77] That's called theme music. A character's theme music might play whenever the character appears on the screen. [94]

Music can change the way you understand a movie even if you're not aware of it. Next time you watch a movie at home, [118] turn off the sound for a minute. Notice the difference that music makes. [131]

KEY NOTES

Music in the Movies
How can music change the way you think during a movie?

_____

_____

Music in the Movies

Music might make a movie scene more exciting.

Fast Facts

- The first movie with recorded sound was *Don Juan*. It had only music, and the actors didn't talk.

- In early movies, a machine called a vitaphone played the music.

- The soundtrack of *Saturday Night Fever* has sold more than 30 million recordings.

Music Sets the Scene

People who make movies use music to help set the scene. A movie director can use music to convey that a movie takes[27] place at a specific time or place. Some kinds of music are easy for an audience to recognize and can help the director create a[52] mood. For example, soft violin music may convey to an audience that a movie is set in a peaceful place.[72]

A movie director can use music to convey other information, too. The sound of drums played in a marching rhythm might be[94] used to convey the idea that characters are going to war. In addition, a chase scene might have music that is played in a[118] fast, exciting rhythm. A movie's music can help explain the action on the screen.[132]

KEY NOTES

Music Sets the Scene

How can music convey information in a movie?

_____

_____

Music in the Movies

Music in a movie may let you know about danger about to happen.

Fast Facts

- String instruments are often used in love scenes.

- Some directors played music when they filmed silent movies to get actors in the right mood.

- Some movie music is made with synthesizers, machines that create music that sounds like an orchestra.

Music Tells the Story

You're watching a movie, and suddenly you feel that something dangerous is about to happen. You might not be[23] conscious of the movie's music, but it may be helping you understand the action you are viewing.[40]

Music might be used to stand for a certain action or mood. If music makes a scene more exciting or shows what characters are feeling, the director is using music to help tell the story.[75]

Even if you're not conscious of it, though, music can help you understand that the characters are feeling happy, sad,[95] excited, scared, or romantic. When you hear romantic music, you are prepared for a scene to be about falling in love. In this[118] way, a movie director can move the plot along with music and with words.[132]

KEY NOTES

Music Tells the Story   Describe the kind of music that might be used in an exciting movie scene.

_____

_____

Music in the Movies

John Williams wrote the music for
Star Wars.

Fast Facts

- John Williams did not plan to work in movies.

- John Williams was 27 when he wrote his first film score.

- Williams wrote the fanfare music for the 1984 summer Olympic Games in Los Angeles.

John Williams

You may never have heard of John Williams. However, you've probably heard his music. John Williams has written[20] music for many popular films, including *Star Wars*, *E.T.*, some of the *Harry Potter* films, and *Jaws*.[37]

Williams was born in New York City, but he and his family moved to California when he was 16. As a young man, Williams[61] studied and played jazz. Later, he moved away from jazz and started writing music for films. Williams has written music for[82] more than 200 films and television programs. He's also written music for international sports competitions.[97]

Over the years, Williams has competed for an Academy Award® more than 35 times and has won five Academy Awards.[117] An Academy Award is perhaps the highest honor people in the film industry can receive.[132]

KEY NOTES
John Williams
Why is John Williams famous?
_____
_____

Music in the Movies

Music in the Movies

1. Music is important in movies because _____

    a. it helps the actors remember what they're supposed to say.
    b. the audience is always aware of it.
    c. it can help the director tell the story.
    d. it keeps people quiet during the movie.

2. This passage is MAINLY about _____

    a. what characters say.
    b. how music is used in movies.
    c. why you should turn off the sound when you watch
       movies at home.
    d. what theme music is.

3. Explain your answer to question 2.

_____

_____

_____

Music Sets the Scene

1. How does music help set the scene in a movie?

    a. It helps make the audience remember the plot of the movie.
    b. It shows how good the musicians are.
    c. It tells about the American West.
    d. It helps the audience understand where and when the movie
       is set.

2. Why would a film about an army have drum music played in a marching rhythm?

_____

_____

_____

3. What kind of music might be played for a scene in which people are running away from an enemy? Why?

_____

_____

_____

Music Tells the Story

1. In this passage, the word _conscious_ means _____

    a. someone is aware of something.
    b. someone is waking up.
    c. someone is playing music you can hear.
    d. someone is telling what a character feels.

2. This passage is MAINLY about _____

    a. music that the characters listen to.
    b. music that helps to tell the story.
    c. music that tells you about danger on the screen.
    d. music that is about falling in love.

3. How does music help a movie director tell the story of the movie?

_____

_____

_____

John Williams

1. What is another good name for "John Williams"?

    a. "The Man Who Makes the Music"
    b. "Winning an Academy Award"
    c. "Music at the Olympics"
    d. "Listening to Music at the Movies"

2. Explain your answer to question 1.

_____

_____

_____

3. How do you think John Williams might have written the music for two different movies listed in this passage?

_____

_____

_____

conscious	rhythm	jazz	director
theme	romantic	convey	Academy Award

1. Choose the word from the word box above that best matches each definition. Write the word on the line below.

A. _____ about feelings of love

B. _____ a tune that is repeated

C. _____ the beat of the music

D. _____ to make someone understand something

E. _____ a person who is in control of making a movie

F. _____ an honor given to people in the movie industry

G. _____ aware of something

H. _____ a style of music

2. Fill in the blank in the sentences below. Choose the word from the word box that completes each sentence.

A. The actor was extremely happy when he won his first

_____.

B. The soft music created a _____ feeling.

C. The director chose a _____ piece for the scene at the night club.

D. We were running because we were _____ that the bus would arrive soon.

E. The quick _____ of the music was perfect for a chase scene.

F. The _____ music for the opening scene was also played at the end of the movie.

G. Slow, soft music was used to _____ the sadness the actress felt.

H. The _____ hired a new musician to write the score for her movie.

Music in the Movies

1. Use the idea web to help you remember what you read. In each box, write the main idea of that passage.

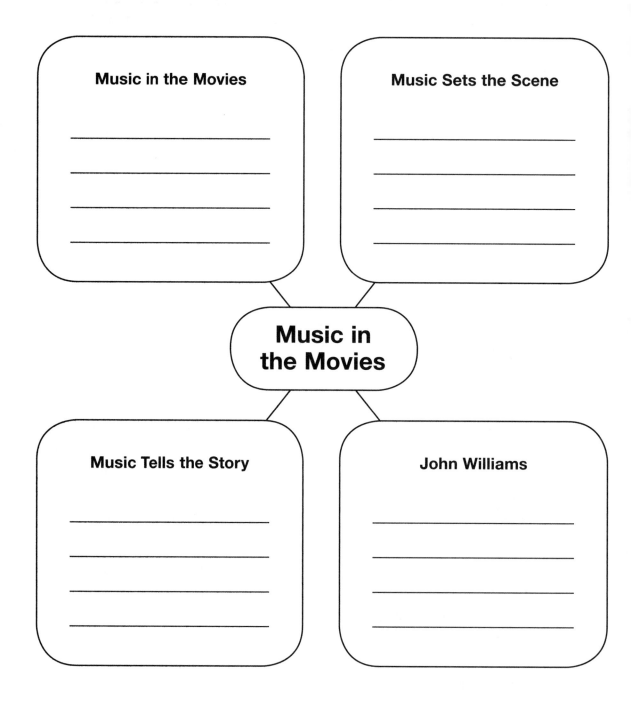

Music in the Movies

Music Sets the Scene

Music in
the Movies

Music Tells the Story

John Williams

2. Tell about three ways you read about in which music can affect the way you feel while you're watching a movie.

_____

_____

_____

_____

3. Describe a time when music in a movie made you feel a certain way.

_____

_____

_____

_____

4. Describe your favorite kind of movie music.

_____

_____

_____

_____

Civil Rights Leaders

All Americans have the same civil rights thanks to leaders like Rosa Parks, shown on a bus in 1955.

Fast Facts

- The United States Constitution was approved in 1788.

- The first 10 amendments to the Constitution, called the Bill of Rights, took effect in 1791.

- There are now 27 amendments to the Constitution.

Civil Rights

In the United States, people have certain private, or civil, rights. Today, people of all races, genders, and religions have[22] civil rights. These rights include the right to vote in elections and to be treated fairly.[38]

When the United States broke away from England, its leaders wrote that "all men are created equal." At that time,[58] however, not everyone in the new nation was treated fairly. Men of some races and women of all races could not vote. They were treated unfairly in other ways, too.[88]

Since that time, amendments have been added to the United States Constitution. These amendments promise civil[104] rights to people of all races, genders, and religions. It wasn't always easy to make these amendments into law. They exist[125] today because some people worked very hard so that all Americans could have the same civil rights.[142]

KEY NOTES

Civil Rights
What are civil rights?

_____

_____

Civil Rights Leaders

Susan B. Anthony spent her life trying to get equal rights for all men and women.

Fast Facts

- Susan B. Anthony was the first woman whose picture appeared on a U.S. coin.

- An amendment giving women the vote was put before each session of Congress from 1878 to 1919.

- The 19th Amendment gave women the right to vote.

Equal Rights for Women

In 1850, Susan B. Anthony was a teacher. At that time, women could not own land or vote, and most African Americans[26] were slaves with no civil rights. Anthony thought this was wrong, so she decided to do whatever she could to win equality for all women and men.[53]

In 1870, the 15th Amendment gave men who had been slaves the right to vote. However, women still did not have this right.[76] Anthony held meetings, gave speeches, and asked people to support women's right to vote. She took 10,000 names of people[96] who wanted equality for women and went to the U.S. Senate. However, the Senate would not listen to her.[115]

When Susan B. Anthony died in 1906, women still were not allowed to vote. However, that changed in 1920, when women finally were given the right to vote.[143]

KEY NOTES

Equal Rights for Women

What did Susan B. Anthony do to help women get the right to vote?

_____

_____

Civil Rights Leaders

In this picture, Thurgood Marshall is sitting on the steps of the U.S. Supreme Court. The students near him gained the right to equal education because of Marshall's work.

Fast Facts

- Thurgood Marshall was born in 1908 and died in 1993.

- Marshall was appointed to the Supreme Court by President Lyndon B. Johnson.

- Marshall was a Supreme Court judge from 1967 to 1991.

Equal Education

In the 1950s, some places in the United States had separate schools for white and black children. Often, white children's[22] schools had better facilities than black children's schools. A lawyer named Thurgood Marshall believed that this was[39] not fair. He argued that because many black children's schools had poor facilities, they did not have the same rights as white children.[62]

Marshall decided to do something about this, so he argued for children's rights to an equal education before the Supreme[82] Court. Marshall argued that all children should have the same education, at the same time, in the same place. The Supreme[103] Court agreed, ruling that separate schools for children of different races were not allowed.[117]

In 1967, Thurgood Marshall became the first African American judge on the Supreme Court. As a Supreme Court judge, Marshall strongly supported equal rights for all people.[144]

KEY NOTES
Equal Education
What did Thurgood Marshall work for?
_____
_____

Civil Rights Leaders

The Voting Rights Act of 1965 is an amendment to the U.S. Constitution that protects everyone's right to vote.

Fast Facts

- Lyndon B. Johnson was born in 1908 and died in 1973.

- Johnson was the 36th president of the United States.

- Johnson was president from 1963 to 1969.

Equal Treatment

Even with amendments to the U.S. Constitution, all people were still not treated equally. Some people were still not allowed[22] to vote. Some people were treated unfairly at work and in public places. President Lyndon B. Johnson, the 36th president of the[44] United States, worked with Congress to pass two acts that made these practices unlawful.[58]

Before the Civil Rights Act of 1964, some businesses and public places refused to serve or hire people because of their[79] race, gender, or religion. The Civil Rights Act of 1964 made such practices unlawful.[93]

Before the Voting Rights Act of 1965, some places required people to pass a reading test or pay a tax to vote. The Voting[117] Rights Act of 1965 made practices like these unlawful. Today, many of our civil rights are protected because President Johnson wanted all Americans to be treated equally.[144]

KEY NOTES

Equal Treatment   Break the word *unlawful* into three parts. How do all three parts help you define the word?

_____   _____   _____

_____

_____

Civil Rights Leaders

Civil Rights

1. The main idea of "Civil Rights" is that _____

    a. the United States was begun by civil rights leaders.
    b. the early leaders of the United States gave civil rights to all people.
    c. people in the United States have the right to vote.
    d. all Americans have civil rights today.

2. In this passage, *gender* means _____

    a. whether someone is old or young.
    b. whether someone is African American or white.
    c. whether someone is male or female.
    d. whether someone is from America or England.

3. What are two civil rights that all people in the United States have today?

_____

_____

_____

Equal Rights for Women

1. In this passage, *equality* means _____

    a. being a male or a female.
    b. having the same rights as others.
    c. having your own land.
    d. being able to vote in elections.

2. What were two rights all people did not have in 1850?

_____

_____

_____

3. Why is Susan B. Anthony called a civil rights leader?

_____

_____

_____

Equal Education

1. Another good name for "Equal Education" is _____

    a. "Schools for Every Town."
    b. "The Supreme Court."
    c. "Thurgood Marshall's Fight."
    d. "Changes at the Supreme Court."

2. Why might children have a better education if they had better school facilities?

_____

_____

_____

3. What was the result of Thurgood Marshall's argument before the Supreme Court?

    a. Black children had white teachers, and white children had black teachers.

    b. Schools for white children were closed in many places.

    c. Separate schools for children of different races became more common.

    d. Separate schools for children of different races were not allowed.

Equal Treatment

1. "Equal Treatment" is MAINLY about _____

    a. how towns passed laws to give everyone civil rights.

    b. laws that made sure all people are treated fairly in the United States.

    c. how businesses refused to serve or hire some people.

    d. why Lyndon B. Johnson became president of the United States.

2. What did the Civil Rights Act of 1964 do?

_____

_____

_____

3. Why is President Lyndon B. Johnson known for his work for civil rights?

_____

_____

_____

| amendments | genders | argued | practices |
| equality | Senate | facilities | unlawful |

1. Choose the word from the word box above that best matches each definition. Write the word on the line below.

A. _____ being men or women

B. _____ against the law

C. _____ gave reasons for or against something

D. _____ the usual ways of doing things

E. _____ one of the parts of the U.S. or state government

F. _____ rooms, supplies, and other things that make things easier to do

G. _____ changes that make things better

H. _____ being the same

2. Fill in the blanks in the sentences below. Choose the word from the word box that completes each sentence.

A. Today, it is _____ to make people pay a tax to vote.

B. Schools that have equal _____ would have the same kinds of books and supplies.

C. Some _____ change the Constitution so that it better protects Americans' rights.

D. Men and women are two _____.

E. During the 1960s, Congress made it _____ to make people pass a reading test to vote.

F. It was many years before the lawmakers in the U.S. _____ gave women the right to vote.

G. When people have complete _____, they can all do the same things.

H. The lawyer _____ that the new law was legal.

Civil Rights Leaders

1. Label the events you read about in the order in which they occurred. Write the letter **A** next to the event that happened first, then arrange the rest of the events in order using **B, C, D, E, F, G,** or **H**.

_____ Women were given the right to vote.

_____ Congress passed an act that said people did not have to pass a reading test or pay a tax to vote.

_____ Thurgood Marshall argued before the Supreme Court for children's rights to an equal education.

_____ Susan B. Anthony went to the U.S. Senate to win women the right to vote.

_____ Congress passed an act that said businesses and public places could not refuse to serve or hire people because of their race, gender, or religion.

_____ The 15th Amendment gave men who had been slaves the right to vote.

_____ Separate schools for children of different races were not allowed.

_____ The U.S. Constitution stated that "all men are created equal."

2. Choose two people you have read about in this topic. Describe why they are called civil rights leaders.

_____

_____

_____

_____

3. What qualities do you think a person needs to have to be called a leader?

_____

_____

_____

_____

4. Do you think there is still more to be done in this country to make sure that all people have the same rights? Explain your answer.

_____

_____

_____

_____

Managing Money

A budget can help you decide how much you need to earn and spend.

Fast Facts

- One Web site lists 12 reasons people should have budgets.

- If you spend $0.75 for a snack every day, you could spend $135 in a year.

- The best way to make a budget is to plan to spend some money on things you need, not just want.

Personal Budgets

A budget is a system for managing money. Families, schools, and businesses all have budgets. Individuals have budgets, too.[21] The difference between budgets for individuals and budgets for businesses is their size. However, no matter what size they are, all budgets have the same two parts.[48]

One part of a budget is a record of income, or money coming in. A teenager's income might include money earned for working[71] at home or at a business. The other part of a budget is a record of expenses, or money going out. A teenager's expenses might include snacks or presents for birthdays.[102]

Individuals and businesses use budgets to manage their money. Records of income and expenses show businesses if they[120] are doing well or poorly. These same records show individuals if they have money to buy things they need or want.[141]

KEY NOTES
Personal Budgets   How can budgets help people manage money?   _____   _____

Managing Money

Jamie has listed her income and her expenses so she can plan her budget.

Creating a Budget

Jamie has a budget that shows her income and expenses for one month. Her income of $25 came from taking care of a[26] neighbor's plants and fish. She also did chores at home every week. Jamie's expenses were $21. Her expenses were three movies, at $7 for each ticket.[52]

The next month, Jamie wanted to buy some computer disks. They cost $6, so she studied her budget. Jamie decided that she[74] could buy the computer disks if she went to one less movie that month and saved the money from the neighbor she would have spent on the ticket.[102]

Then, she remembered that her mother's birthday was the next month. Jamie decided that she would go to only two[122] movies that month. That way, she could buy the computer disks and still have money to buy her mother a birthday gift.[144]

KEY NOTES

Creating a Budget
How did Jamie find out how much money she could spend?

_____

_____

Managing Money

This bank helps people invest money in savings or stocks.

Fast Facts

- In 2005, there were more than 91,000 banks in the United States.

- In 2005, U.S. banks held a total of $5.9 trillion.

- In 2005, close to 2,800 companies were listed on the New York Stock Exchange.

Investing Money

If a person leaves $20 in a drawer for one year, he or she will have $20 at the end of the year. Money left in a drawer[30] does not increase in value. To increase in value, money must be invested.[43]

The easiest way to invest money is to put it in a savings account at a bank. Banks pay interest on savings accounts. With a 5% interest rate, $20 will be worth $21 after one year.[79]

Stocks are another way to invest money. A company that needs money can sell shares of its business. These shares are[100] called stocks. Stocks can increase or decrease in value. If a company makes money, a $20 stock could be worth $50 in one[123] year. However, if a company loses money, a $20 stock could decrease in value and be worth only $5.[142]

KEY NOTES

Investing Money

What are two ways people can invest their money?

_____

_____

Managing Money

Government revenues are used to pay for new roads.

Fast Facts

- In 2004, revenue for the United States was about $1.9 trillion.

- In 2004, expenses for the United States were about $2.3 trillion.

- In 2004, the U.S. government earned about $809 billion from people's income taxes.

Government Budgets

Like people, governments have budgets with two parts: income, or revenue, and expenses. Governments earn revenue[18] from taxes. The U.S. government earns revenue by taxing the income people earn from jobs and from selling goods. Many[38] states earn revenue by adding a sales tax to the goods people buy. City governments earn revenue from sales taxes and[59] property taxes. Property taxes are paid by people who own houses, stores, or other property.[74]

Part of a government's expenses are the services it provides. These services cost money. The U.S. government's expenses[92] include the armed forces. A state government's expenses include roads and schools. A local government's expenses include fire and police services.[113]

Like people, governments have to manage their budgets. If they don't, they could go into debt. Staying out of debt is one reason people and governments make—and keep—budgets.[143]

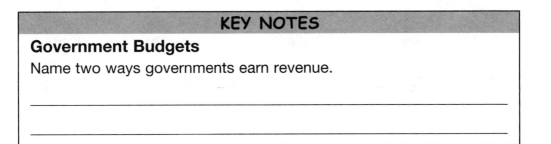

KEY NOTES

Government Budgets

Name two ways governments earn revenue.

_____

_____

113

Managing Money

Personal Budgets

1. A budget is a system for _____

    a. doing jobs for businesses.
    b. earning money.
    c. saving money.
    d. managing money.

2. What is income?

    a. money that is being spent
    b. money that is being earned
    c. money that belongs to someone else
    d. money that must be paid to a bank

3. Describe the two parts of a budget.

_____

_____

_____

Creating a Budget

1. Jamie's income is from _____

    a. taking care of a neighbor's plants and fish and doing chores
       at school.
    b. spending money on movies and taking care of a neighbor's dog.
    c. taking care of a neighbor's plants and fish and doing chores
       at home.
    d. buying birthday gifts and selling movie tickets.

2. Why does Jamie want to know the difference between her income and her expenses?

_____

_____

_____

3. How does Jamie plan her budget for the month?

_____

_____

_____

Investing Money

1. "Investing Money" is MAINLY about _____

    a. why you should leave money in a drawer.
    b. ways to invest money.
    c. why companies sell stocks.
    d. ways to invest money in a bank.

2. Why will money increase in value if you put it in a savings account?

_____

_____

_____

3. What can happen to your money if you invest it in stocks?

_____

_____

_____

Government Budgets

1. The main idea of "Government Budgets" is that _____

    a. governments provide services.
    b. both governments and people have budgets.
    c. governments invest their money in taxes.
    d. governments get their revenue from savings.

2. One way governments earn revenue is from _____

    a. services.
    b. taxes.
    c. budgets.
    d. police.

3. How are the budgets of governments and people alike?

_____

_____

_____

debt	budget	decrease	expenses	neighbor
invest	revenue	ticket	increase	

1. Choose the word from the word box above that best matches each definition. Write the word on the line below.

A. _____ a paper or card that shows that money has been paid for a service

B. _____ money that must be paid to someone

C. _____ money that is taken in by a government

D. _____ a system for managing money

E. _____ to go up in value

F. _____ to go down in value

G. _____ owing someone money

H. _____ to manage money so that it might grow in value

I. _____ someone who lives nearby

2. Fill in the blanks in the sentences below. Choose the word from the word box that completes each sentence.

A. The price of a movie ticket may _____ if movies cost more to make.

B. We will _____ money in stocks, so we might have more money next year.

C. John lists how much he spends in his _____.

D. Alex paid $10 for a _____ to the new movie.

E. My _____, who lives next door, likes to walk my dog.

F. Because Ellen keeps a _____, she knows how much to spend.

G. When the company lost money, its stock began to _____.

H. The government built new roads using tax _____.

I. Mark spent more than he earned, so he is now in _____.

117

Managing Money

1. Use the chart to help you remember what you read. Fill in a cause or an effect in the empty boxes.

Cause	Effect
A.	You do chores for your neighbors.
B. You buy snacks at school every day.	
C. You want something, but don't have enough money in your budget.	
D.	You have extra money at the end of the month.
E. You put $10 in a drawer and leave it there for a year.	
F.	A company raises the prices of the things it sells.
G. A government taxes income and goods.	
H.	A government goes into debt.

2. What are two things you could do if your budget did not balance?

_____

_____

_____

_____

3. Why is it important for people, businesses, and governments to manage money?

_____

_____

_____

_____

4. What might happen if people, businesses, and governments don't manage their money well?

_____

_____

_____

_____

The American Civil War

Before and during the U.S. Civil War, much of the South's money was earned through slavery.

Fast Facts

- The American Civil War began on April 12, 1861.

- The first state to leave the Union was South Carolina.

- The president of the Confederate States was Jefferson Davis.

The Civil War Begins

Although the United States was less than 100 years old, it was a troubled country. The South's income came mostly from[25] cotton farming. Cotton was cheap to grow if enslaved people worked the fields. The North's income came from businesses that did not use slavery, including banks and railroads.[53]

When the United States was formed, five of the 13 states demanded that slavery remain legal. As new states were added,[74] the North and South argued about whether slavery should be legal in these places.[88]

In 1860, the South believed that President Lincoln would make slavery illegal, so 11 states formed their own country,[107] which they called the Confederate States of America. The 23 remaining states were called the Union. In 1861, the Confederate[127] States and the Union could not agree on slavery and other things, so they went to war.[144]

KEY NOTES

The Civil War Begins

What were the two sides in the Civil War?

_____

_____

The American Civil War

This painting shows the Union and Confederate armies fighting during the Battle of Gettysburg.

Fast Facts

- The Battle of Gettysburg began on July 1, 1863.

- More than 600,000 soldiers died during the American Civil War.

- Lincoln's famous Gettysburg Address is fewer than 300 words long.

The Battle of Gettysburg

In the spring of 1861, the Confederate army fired on a Union fort, and the Civil War began. Most of the fighting took[27] place in the Confederate states or in Union states that allowed slavery. However, in July 1863, the South's army invaded the[48] North. Two large armies, one Southern and one Northern, met at Gettysburg, Pennsylvania. During the three days of fighting, about 51,000 soldiers died.[71]

The Battle of Gettysburg was a turning point in the war. After that Pennsylvania battle, the Confederate army did not invade the North again.[95]

In November 1863, President Lincoln gave a speech at Gettysburg to honor the soldiers of both armies who had[114] fought and died there. He ended his speech by saying that a "government of the people, by the people, for the people, shall not perish from the Earth."[142]

KEY NOTES

The Battle of Gettysburg
Who did President Lincoln honor at Gettysburg?

_____

_____

The American Civil War

This picture shows a group of Union soldiers in New York in 1861.

Fast Facts

- About 2,100,000 soldiers served in the Union army.

- About 800,000 soldiers served in the Confederate army.

- About 200,000 African Americans fought for the Union.

Civil War Soldiers

Union soldiers wore blue uniforms, and Confederate soldiers wore gray uniforms. At first, soldiers in both armies[20] had enough food and weapons. However, as the war went on, the Confederacy began to run out of supplies. Some Confederate soldiers could not even get shoes.[47]

Many freed and runaway slaves enlisted in, or joined, the Union army. However, even though they were free, African[66] American soldiers were not treated well. They were not allowed to fight with white soldiers. They were given old uniforms[86] and weapons that were in poor condition. Even so, African Americans enlisted in the army and fought hard for the Union.[107]

More American lives were lost in the Civil War than in any other war the United States has ever fought. By the time the[131] fighting stopped, more than one million soldiers had died or were wounded.[143]

KEY NOTES

Civil War Soldiers

How were the Union army and the Confederate army different?

_____

_____

The American Civil War

This painting shows General Lee's surrender to General Grant. The states came together again to rebuild the United States.

Fast Facts

- Robert E. Lee surrendered on April 9, 1865.

- Abraham Lincoln was killed on April 14, 1865.

- About 360,000 Union soldiers and 260,000 Confederate soldiers died in the war.

After the War

In April 1865, General Lee, the leader of the Confederate army, surrendered to General Grant, the leader of the Union[23] army. General Grant told the Union soldiers not to celebrate but to treat the Confederate soldiers as their fellow Americans.[43]

The nation also did not celebrate the end of the war. Less than a week after the South surrendered, President Lincoln was[65] killed by a Southerner who was angry that the Confederacy lost the war. Although President Lincoln had saved the Union, he did not live to bring the nation together again.[95]

After the war, the South faced many problems. It needed new sources of income. The land had not been farmed, so there[117] was little food. Although slavery was now illegal, people of different races did not get along. It took the United States many years to heal.[142]

KEY NOTES

After the War

How did General Grant want the Union soldiers to act after the war?

_____

_____

The American Civil War

The Civil War Begins

1. How did the North and the South get their income before the Civil War?

    a. The North's income came from slavery, but the South's did not.
    b. Both the North and the South got their income from banks and cotton.
    c. The South's income came from slavery, but the North's did not.
    d. Both the North and the South got their incomes from the Union.

2. Compare what people in the North and the South thought about slavery.

_____

_____

_____

3. Why did the Southern states form the Confederate States of America?

_____

_____

_____

The Battle of Gettysburg

1. At Gettysburg, President Lincoln gave a speech that honored all of the soldiers who fought _____

    a. in the Civil War.
    b. for the Union army.
    c. and died at Gettysburg.
    d. for the Confederate army.

2. What did President Lincoln say about government in his speech at Gettysburg?

_____

_____

_____

3. Why was the Battle of Gettysburg important?

_____

_____

_____

Civil War Soldiers

1. Which of the following was true of soldiers during the Civil War?

    a. Soldiers on both sides always had enough supplies.

    b. African American soldiers were not treated well.

    c. Many freed and runaway slaves enlisted in the Confederate army.

    d. All of the soldiers had blue uniforms, rifles, and backpacks.

2. As the war went on _____

    a. more Union soldiers joined the Confederate army.

    b. the Confederacy began to run out of supplies.

    c. few African American soldiers enlisted in the army.

    d. the Union army began to run out of supplies.

3. How were African American soldiers treated in the Union army?

_____

_____

_____

After the War

"After the War" is MAINLY about _____

    a. how the United States healed after the Civil War.
    b. why General Lee surrendered to General Grant.
    c. why President Lincoln was killed.
    d. what happened when the Civil War was over.

2. Why do you think General Grant told the Union soldiers not to celebrate winning the Civil War?

_____

_____

_____

3. What problems did the South have after the war?

_____

_____

_____

| celebrate | invaded | Gettysburg | slavery | enlist |
| Confederate | surrendered | weapons | Pennsylvania | |

1. Choose the word from the word box above that best matches each definition. Write the word on the line below.

A. _____ to join the armed forces

B. _____ a place where a famous Civil War battle was fought

C. _____ to make a certain day or thing special

D. _____ part of the name of the country formed by the 11 states that left the Union

E. _____ gave up

F. _____ things used to defend or attack someone

G. _____ entered an area to take control of it

H. _____ the condition of a person who is held and forced to work by another

I. _____ the name of a state in the United States

2. Fill in the blanks in the sentences below. Choose the word from the word box that completes each sentence.

A. The war began when the army _____ the other country.

B. The soldiers' _____ were used to kill people in the war.

C. The Battle of _____ was a turning point in the American Civil War.

D. After the losing army _____, the fighting stopped.

E. Maria won a medal, so we decided to _____.

F. President Lincoln gave a famous speech in Gettysburg, _____.

G. When the Southern states left the Union, they formed the _____ States of America.

H. _____ was one cause of the American Civil War.

I. Last week, Richard decided to _____ in the air force.

131

The American Civil War

1. Use the idea web to help you remember what you read. For each
box, write two important facts from that passage.

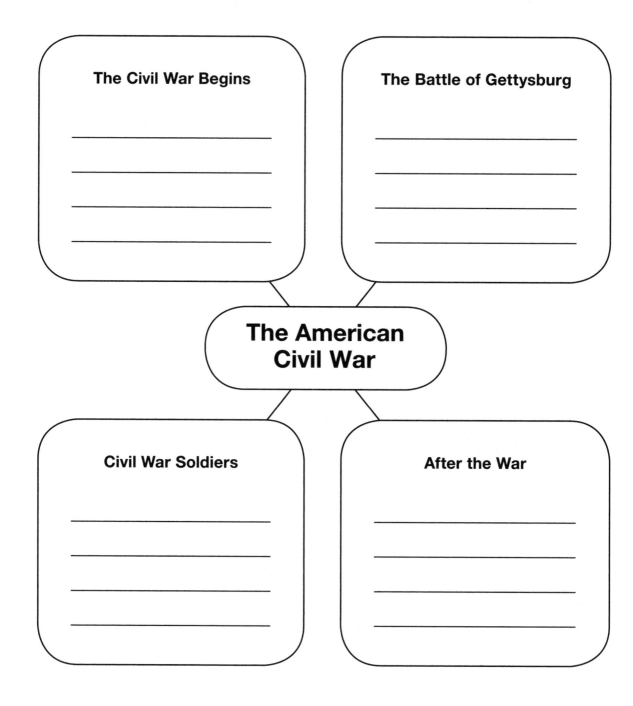

The Civil War Begins

The Battle of Gettysburg

**The American
Civil War**

Civil War Soldiers

After the War

2. How was the Civil War different from other wars the United States has fought?

_____

_____

_____

_____

3. Do you think we have a "government of the people, by the people, for the people" today? Explain.

_____

_____

_____

_____

4. Suppose it was your job to bring the North and the South together after the Civil War. Tell about three things you would do.

_____

_____

_____

_____

Science Fiction

Science fiction stories are often in the future.

Fast Facts

- Mary Shelley is called the Mother of Science Fiction because her book, *Frankenstein* (1818), is the first science fiction novel.

- In 1863, the writer Jules Verne predicted televisions, submarines, and cars.

- Science fiction is sometimes called "Sci-Fi."

What Is Science Fiction?

Imagine a man facing a pack of hungry space aliens. Then, imagine a girl shrinking to the size of a dime. Finally, imagine[27] people who try to read books, but firefighters take their books and then arrest them. Events like these occur in science fiction.[49]

Science fiction stories are often strange tales that have roots in science. It is the science in science fiction that makes these stories seem like they could happen.[77]

There are different kinds of science fiction. Travel stories might include trips into the past or the future, or into outer[98] space. Alien stories might include creatures that invade Earth. Sometimes, however, the aliens are humans who land on[116] other planets. Another kind of science fiction might include civilizations that seem perfect, but have hidden secrets. Science[134] fiction writers create stories that amaze us and also make us think about our own world.[150]

KEY NOTES

What Is Science Fiction?
What are science fiction stories about?

_____

_____

Science Fiction

These people love to read stories by Ray Bradbury. They attended an event in Hollywood that honored the author.

Fast Facts

- Ray Bradbury was born in Waukegan, Illinois, on August 22, 1920.

- Bradbury wrote his first story when he was 12 years old.

- Dandelion Crater on the moon is named after Bradbury's book *Dandelion Wine*.

Ray Bradbury

Ray Bradbury is one of the greatest writers of science fiction, and he has won many honors for his work. Several things inspired Ray Bradbury to write science fiction.[31]

As a child, Bradbury was interested in magic. When he was 11 years old, he saw a performance by Harry Blackstone,[52] a famous magician. Bradbury even went up on stage to help Blackstone make a horse disappear. From that time, Bradbury loved magic.[74]

Movies, adventure books, and comic strips also inspired Ray Bradbury. He especially liked horror films filled with[91] mystery and with unusual and strange creatures. His favorite adventures took place on other worlds. In the daily newspapers, he read comic strips that had ray guns and rocket ships.[121]

Bradbury creates magic through words. His stories take readers on trips through space and time. He tells tales of strange[141] beings and surprising events that sometimes seem both scary and real.[152]

KEY NOTES

Ray Bradbury
What does Ray Bradbury write about?

_____

_____

Science Fiction

This scene from the movie *Fahrenheit 451* shows books burning.

Fast Facts

- Ray Bradbury wrote the first draft of *Fahrenheit 451* in nine days.

- *Fahrenheit 451* was published in 1953 and was made into a movie in 1966.

- In *Fahrenheit 451*, Bradbury predicted headset radios, wall-sized TV screens, and reality programs.

Fahrenheit 451

Fahrenheit 451 is Ray Bradbury's most popular science fiction book. The story takes place in a future in which books[22] and reading are against the law. When books are discovered, they're burned and their owners are arrested. The temperature at which books burn is 451° Fahrenheit.[48]

In this future, firefighters don't put out fires. Instead, they make fires and burn books. Guy Montag is a firefighter who[69] questions the purpose of his job. Because he secretly reads books, Montag begins to understand how books can lead people to ask[91] questions about things that are going on around them. He comes to realize that his government doesn't want people to think.[112]

When Montag's reading is discovered, officers try to arrest him. However, Montag escapes and joins a group of people who[132] are trying to save books by memorizing them. Later, they'll tell their memorized books to others so that books won't be forgotten.[154]

KEY NOTES

Fahrenheit 451
In *Fahrenheit 451*, what happens to people who read?

_____

_____

Science Fiction

Ray Bradbury wrote the book
Fahrenheit 451.

Fast Facts

- Censored books are also known as banned books.
- Some groups have burned *Harry Potter* books.
- *Fahrenheit 451*'s publisher censored the book in 98 places.

Censorship

One of the main ideas in *Fahrenheit 451* is that people have a right to read books, even if others don't like the ideas in[26] them. When people are not allowed to read what others have written, it is called censorship. Sometimes some of the words are changed. At other times, a whole book is censored.[57]

At times, *Fahrenheit 451* itself was censored. In 1967, the book's publisher began to sell a version of the book in which words that might offend some readers were changed, or edited.[89]

In 1979, Ray Bradbury discovered that only the edited version of *Fahrenheit 451* was available. He was angry that the[109] book in which he wrote about the danger of censorship was itself being censored. Because he wanted people to read his book[131] as he had written it, Ray Bradbury ordered the publisher to sell *Fahrenheit 451* only in its original, unedited version.[151]

KEY NOTES

Censorship
What is censorship?

_____

_____

Science Fiction

What Is Science Fiction?

1. This passage is MAINLY about _____

    a. people who write science fiction.
    b. different kinds of science fiction.
    c. stories that take place in the future.
    d. stories that have unhappy endings.

2. Explain your answer to question 1.

_____

_____

_____

3. In this passage, *alien* means _____

_____

_____

_____

Ray Bradbury

1. Another good name for "Ray Bradbury" is _____

    a. "The Magic Show."
    b. "A Science Fiction Writer's Life."
    c. "Magic and Science Fiction Movies."
    d. "Traveling Through Space and Time."

2. In this passage, *inspire* means _____

    a. to write books and stories.
    b. to create magic through words.
    c. to read books and comic strips.
    d. to cause someone to do something.

3. What inspired Ray Bradbury to write science fiction?

_____

_____

_____

Fahrenheit 451

1. Why is it against the law to read in *Fahrenheit 451*?

    a. The government doesn't want people to think.
    b. Books catch fire very easily, so it isn't safe to read.
    c. Guy Montag doesn't want people to think.
    d. The firefighters want people to be safe.

2. In *Fahrenheit 451*, people try to save books by _____

    a. becoming firefighters.
    b. arresting Montag.
    c. putting out fires.
    d. memorizing them.

3. Tell what the book *Fahrenheit 451* is about.

_____

_____

_____

Censorship

1. This passage is MAINLY about _____

    a. why *Fahrenheit 451* was censored.
    b. how some books are censored.
    c. the censorship of *Fahrenheit 451*.
    d. what censorship is.

2. In this passage, *edit* means _____

_____

_____

_____

3. Do you think it could be right to censor books? Explain your answer.

_____

_____

_____

fiction	alien	inspired	Fahrenheit
memorize	censored	edited	strange

1. Choose the word from the word box above that best matches each definition. Write the word on the line below.

A. _____ a scale for measuring temperature

B. _____ readings with characters and events that were created by a writer

C. _____ to learn something so that it can be repeated exactly

D. _____ made someone want to do something

E. _____ took out information so that others cannot read or see it

F. _____ from another world

G. _____ unusual, uncommon

H. _____ to change words in something

2. Fill in the blanks in the sentences below. Choose the word from the word box that completes each sentence.

A. An _____ that looked like a giant ape landed on Earth.

B. I read a book of _____ that had characters that sounded like my friends.

C. The official _____ the book to keep some people's names secret.

D. Water will boil at 212 degrees _____.

E. I need to _____ the script before the first performance of the play.

F. I _____ my paper to add more information about the topic.

G. Your music was so exciting it _____ me to start singing again.

H. The science fiction novel had a _____ character in it.

Science Fiction

1. Use the idea web to help you remember what you read. In each box, write the main idea of that reading. Then, use that information to write the main idea of the topic.

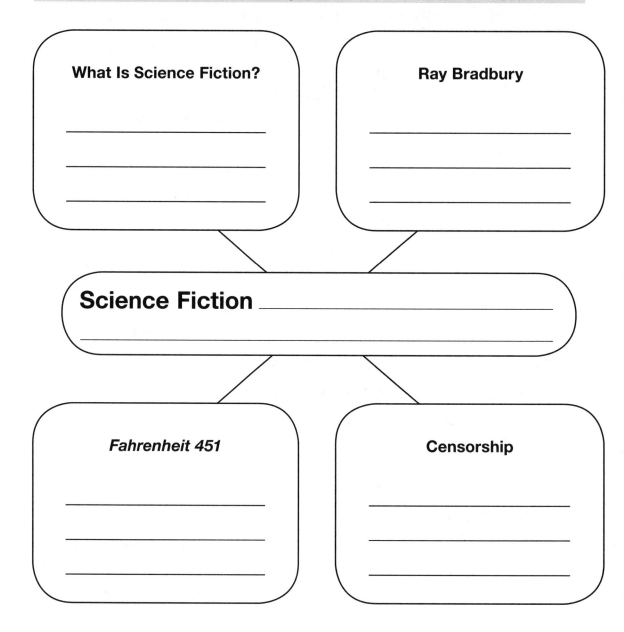

What Is Science Fiction?

_____

_____

_____

Ray Bradbury

_____

_____

_____

Science Fiction _____

_____

Fahrenheit 451

_____

_____

_____

Censorship

_____

_____

_____

2. What are some of the kinds of science fiction stories?

_____

_____

_____

_____

3. Why do you think certain books might be censored or banned?

_____

_____

_____

_____

4. How would you explain science fiction to someone who didn't know about it?

_____

_____

_____

_____

All About English

This painting shows people from France coming to England in 1066.

Fast Facts

- English has more words than any other language.

- The largest English dictionaries have more than 600,000 words.

- English is the native language of about 400 million people around the world.

English Roots

Many years ago, the language that became English was spoken by groups of people who lived in the area that today is[24] called England. One group was the Angles. The name *England* comes from a word meaning "land of the Angles."[43]

Some words, like *man* and *sun*, were already part of the Angles' language. However, this language evolved as it became[63] English. As English evolved, words were borrowed from other languages. *History*, for example, was borrowed from Greek.[80]

During the late 800s, people from northern Europe called the Vikings invaded England. Then, words from the Vikings'[98] languages became part of English. In 1066, a group from France conquered England. Once the English nobles learned French, French words also became part of English.[124]

Many English words come from Latin and Greek. *Bio* is from a Greek word meaning "life." English words containing *bio*, such as *biology*, have to do with living things.[153]

KEY NOTES

English Roots
How did the English language evolve?

_____

_____

All About English

DANGER
HIGH
VOLTAGE

PELIGRO
ALTO
VOLTAJE

Words from Latin are found in the English and Spanish languages.

Fast Facts

- In some U.S. cities, a language called Spanglish combines Spanish and English.

- *Nueva* means *new* in Spanish, so *Nueva York* means *New York* in Spanish.

- Spanish has been called the second most important U.S. language after English.

English and Spanish Words

Some languages, such as Spanish, have words that closely resemble English words. In fact, some Spanish words resemble[22] English words so closely that it is easy to know what they mean even if you don't speak Spanish.[41]

For example, look at the Spanish words *artista* and *fantástico*. It is not hard to see what they mean in English—*artist*[63] and *fantastic*. Both of these examples are altered only at the end of the word.[78]

Sometimes words are altered in the middle. If you look at the Spanish word *nación*, it is not hard to figure out that the word means *nation* in English.[107]

The reason that English and Spanish words can be so similar is that both languages have many words that came from[128] Latin. Each language has altered the words a little. However, because the words have not changed completely, you can still recognize them.[150]

KEY NOTES

English and Spanish Words
Why do some English and Spanish words look similar?

_____

_____

All About English

To "let the cat out of the bag" is an English idiom for telling a secret.

Fast Facts

- At least four English idioms refer to apples.

- One modern English idiom is "24/7," which means "24 hours a day, 7 days a week."

- The English idiom "break a leg" means "good luck" to actors.

Idioms

Has anyone ever told you to "keep your shirt on" or asked you not to "beat around the bush"? Do you think that some[25] things are as "easy as pie"? Did you ever "learn something by heart"? These expressions are called idioms. An idiom is an[47] expression that means something other than what the words actually mean.[58]

Every language has idioms. People who speak that language know what these expressions mean. However, idioms don't[75] always translate well into other languages. The English idiom "let the cat out of the bag" means "reveal a secret." Spanish[96] has an idiom that means the same thing. When you translate it into English, it means "the cake was discovered." If a Spanish-[119] speaking person said that to nonspeakers, they might ask, "What cake?"[130]

Idioms can be hard to understand when you don't know a language. However, they make language interesting because they paint pictures with words.[153]

KEY NOTES

Idioms
What are idioms?

_____

_____

All About English

New English words, like *soul patch* for a small beard, happen every day.

Fast Facts

- The first sandwich was beef between two slices of toasted bread.

- *Television* comes from *tele*, which means "distant," and *vision*, which means "see."

- *Cell phone* entered the language in 1984.

New English Words

English is always changing. One way it changes is by adding new words. These words are created in several ways.[23] Some words come from words we already have. *Splashdown* is a combination of *splash* and *down*. *Smog* is a combination of *smoke* and *fog.*[47]

Some words come from the names of people or places. Before 1762, the word *sandwich* didn't refer to food. At that time[69] a British noble, the Earl of Sandwich, asked for some meat between two slices of bread. This type of food became known as a sandwich.[94]

Many new words come from science because we need to name new things. After a way was created to send mail through[116] computers, the new mail needed a name. That is how the word *e-mail,* or electronic mail, became an English word. The word[138] *smog* was created to name a problem that happened when fog mixed with smoky fumes.[153]

KEY NOTES
New English Words
Why are words added to English?
_____
_____

All About English

English Roots

1. Two groups of people that invaded England were _____

    a. the Vikings and the English.
    b. the French and the Russians.
    c. the French and the Spanish.
    d. the Vikings and the French.

2. As English evolved, _____

    a. it had fewer and fewer words.
    b. it borrowed words from other languages.
    c. it began to sound like the Vikings' languages.
    d. it lost words that came from Greek.

3. Summarize what you have learned about the English language in this passage.

_____

_____

_____

English and Spanish Words

1. In this passage, *altered* means _____

    a. changed.
    b. at the end.
    c. in the middle.
    d. artistic.

2. What is the main idea of "English and Spanish Words"?

_____

_____

_____

3. How might you be able to read words in a language you can't speak?

_____

_____

_____

Idioms

1. When you use an idiom, _____

    a. you say something different from what the words mean.

    b. you use an expression that no one will understand.

    c. you use an expression that means something different to everyone.

    d. you say something that will make people laugh.

2. Explain what the Spanish idiom "the cake was discovered" means.

_____

_____

_____

157

3. What is the meaning of the English idiom "let the cat out of the bag"?

_____

_____

_____

New English Words

1. Another good name for "New English Words" is _____

    a. "English Names."
    b. "Expanding English."
    c. "People, Places, and Things."
    d. "Smog and E-mail."

2. How did the word _smog_ come into English?

_____

_____

_____

3. The word _e-mail_ means _____

    a. extra mail.
    b. electronic mail.
    c. English mail.
    d. extra mail.

evolved	Vikings	resemble	altered
idiom	translate	smog	e-mail

1. Choose the word from the word box above that best matches each definition. Write the word on the line below.

A. _____ people who lived in northern Europe

B. _____ an expression that means something other than what its words say

C. _____ a combination of smoke and fog

D. _____ messages sent by computer

E. _____ change a word in one language into a word in another language

F. _____ made different

G. _____ to look like something or someone

H. _____ slowly changed

2. Fill in the blanks in the sentences below. Choose the word from the word box that completes each sentence.

A. Some expressions don't _____ easily from one language to another.

B. Hundreds of years ago, England was invaded by the _____.

C. The English _____ "take a hike" means "go away."

D. I hardly _____ my essay between the first and final drafts.

E. Alex checked his _____ to see if he had new messages.

F. _____ can make breathing hard in many cities today.

G. English has _____ to be quite different from the way it was at first.

H. There are words in English and Spanish that closely _____ each other.

All About English

1. Use the idea web to help you remember what you read. In each
box, write the main idea of that reading.

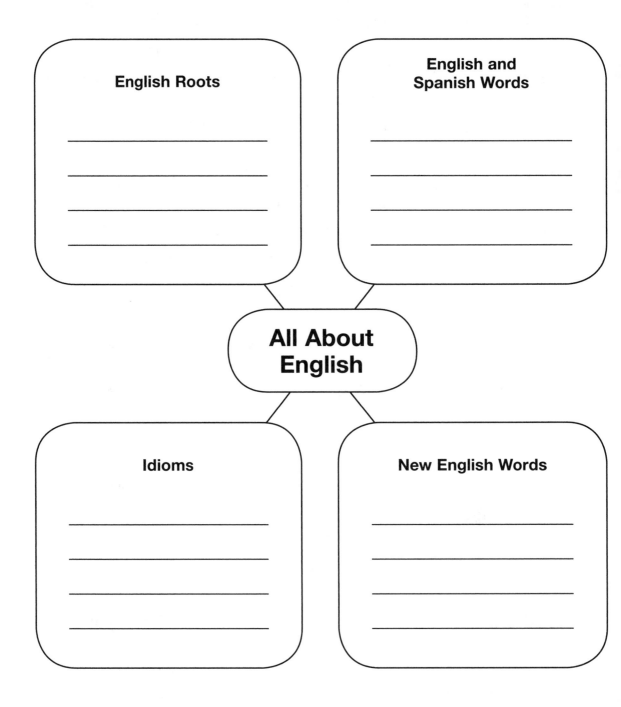

English Roots

_____

_____

_____

_____

**English and
Spanish Words**

_____

_____

_____

_____

All About
English

Idioms

_____

_____

_____

_____

New English Words

_____

_____

_____

_____

2. How has English changed over the years?

_____

_____

_____

_____

3. Why does English keep changing?

_____

_____

_____

_____

4. How do you think English might change in the future?

_____

_____

_____

_____

Newspapers

This special press rolls out the news on newsprint paper.

Fast Facts

- The first newspapers were probably handwritten newssheets that were posted in public places.

- The earliest known daily newssheet appeared in Rome in 59 B.C.

- The first printed newspaper appeared in China in the A.D. 700s.

Publishing a Newspaper

There are many steps involved in publishing a newspaper. First, the stories are written. Then, the pages of the newspaper[23] are created. This is done by making a layout of each page. A layout is a pattern that shows where each story will appear on each page.[50]

When the layouts are finished, a printing plate is made for each page. Many newspapers are printed on a machine called a[72] rotary press. A rotary press has cylinders. These cylinders hold curved printing plates. The cylinders transfer the images that are on the plates to a special paper called newsprint.[101]

From the rotary press, the newspapers go to other machines. One machine cuts the paper and folds it into pages. Another puts[123] the newspaper together. Finally, trucks deliver the papers to newsstands and to other locations where they are picked up by people who deliver the papers to homes.[150]

KEY NOTES

Publishing a Newspaper
What are some of the main steps in publishing a newspaper?

_____

_____

Newspapers

Many students read newspapers at school.

Fast Facts

- Today, the United States has about 1,500 daily newspapers.

- In 2003, U.S. residents bought more than 54 million newspapers every day.

- In 2003, U.S. residents recycled more than 73 percent of their old newspapers.

What's in a Newspaper?

Newspapers are organized into sections to help people find stories that interest them. Two popular sections are news and[23] sports. The sports section reports on the scores, teams, and players in different sports.[37]

Many newspapers have several news sections. The international news section reports on events around the world.[53] The national news section reports on events around the nation. The state news section reports on events in the state. The local[75] news section reports on events in the city. Some newspapers call this the metropolitan news section.[91]

One popular type of story, which is found throughout a newspaper, is the feature story. Feature stories report on topics[111] such as art, technology, and health. They also report on people or places in the metropolitan area. Although they tell about[132] recent trends, feature stories are not like news in that they don't have to be printed as soon as they are written.[154]

KEY NOTES

What's in a Newspaper?
What are the sections in a newspaper?

_____

_____

Newspapers

Newspapers contain opinions about issues that students care about.

Fast Facts

- The opinion page is called the op-ed page, which means "opposite the editorial page."

- Some editorial pages have political cartoons and editorial articles.

- The opinion articles in newspapers might help readers form their own opinions on issues.

That's Your Opinion

In addition to reporting on the news, newspapers tell what people think about the news. Movie reviews are popular feature[23] stories in newspapers. Movie reviews tell what movies are about and what reviewers liked and didn't like about them. They also[44] give the reviewers' opinions about whether films are worth seeing. Newspapers also review books, plays, and TV shows.[62]

The editorial page prints the newspaper's opinion on important issues. Although news sections present only the facts[79] about an issue, editorial pages present editors' opinions about the issue. The page that is opposite the editorial page often prints[100] articles by experts who present their opinions on important issues. These experts' opinions may be different from the opinions of the newspaper's staff.[123]

Many newspapers print readers' opinions on the letters page. The letters might contain people's opinions about things that they've read in the paper or about events in the news.[152]

KEY NOTES

That's Your Opinion
Where do newspapers print opinions?

_____

_____

Newspapers

Newspaper circulation begins early in the day.

The Newspaper Business

To stay in business, newspapers must make enough money to pay their bills. Newspapers earn a large amount of money[23] by selling ads. Advertising income is necessary for the finances of most newspapers. Some ads are for stores, products, services,[43] or jobs. People who want to sell homes or cars also buy newspaper ads.[57]

Businesses and people pay newspapers to publish their ads. How much newspapers charge for ads depends on the[75] paper's circulation. Circulation refers to how many copies of a newspaper are sold. Like advertising, circulation is an important[94] part of a newspaper's finances. Papers with a high circulation have many readers, so more people see their ads. These[114] newspapers can charge more for their ads and earn more money. Papers with a low circulation have fewer readers, so they must[136] charge less for ads. Newspapers hire people who sell advertising space, allowing newspapers to keep printing the news.[154]

KEY NOTES

The Newspaper Business
Describe one way newspapers make money.

_____

_____

Newspapers

Publishing a Newspaper

1. A newspaper layout is _____

    a. a pattern that shows where each story will appear.
    b. a machine that is used to print newspapers.
    c. a pattern that shows where the photographs will appear.
    d. a machine that cuts and folds newspapers.

2. Another good name for "Publishing a Newspaper" is _____

    a. "How Newspapers Are Delivered."
    b. "Working for a Newspaper."
    c. "How Newspapers Are Created."
    d. "Printing a Newspaper."

3. This passage is MAINLY about _____.

_____

_____

_____

What's in a Newspaper?

1. Newspapers are organized in sections to make it easier _____

    a. to create layouts for newspapers.
    b. for people to find stories they want to read.
    c. for writers to know which stories to write.
    d. all of the above

2. In which part of a newspaper would you find an article about the queen of England?

    a. local news
    b. state news
    c. national news
    d. international news

3. What are feature stories?

_____

_____

_____

That's Your Opinion

1. The newspaper page that is opposite the editorial page often prints _____

    a. the newspaper's opinions about important issues.
    b. reviews of movies, books, plays, and TV shows.
    c. letters that contain readers' opinions about the news.
    d. experts' opinions on important issues.

2. What is the difference between a news report and an editorial opinion on an issue?

_____

_____

_____

3. Why do you think newspapers publish opinions?

_____

_____

_____

The Newspaper Business

1. Another good name for "The Newspaper Business" is _____

    a. "How to Write a Newspaper Ad."
    b. "Using a Newspaper to Sell a Car."
    c. "Why Newspapers Print Ads."
    d. "How Newspapers Raise Their Circulation."

2. Why are ads important to newspapers?

_____

_____

_____

3. Why can newspapers with a high circulation charge more for their ads?

_____

_____

_____

circulation	cylinders	editorial	feature
finances	metropolitan	review	rotary

1. Choose the word from the word box above that matches each definition. Write the word on the line below.

A. _____ a person's, government's, or business's money

B. _____ turning in a circle

C. _____ having to do with a city

D. _____ a kind of story that doesn't have to be printed as soon as it's written

E. _____ an article that gives an opinion about a movie, book, or play

F. _____ long, round tubes

G. _____ an article that gives a newspaper's opinion on an issue

H. _____ the number of copies of a newspaper that are sold

2. Fill in the blanks in the sentences below. Choose the word from the word box that completes each sentence.

A. The newspaper's _____ section prints news from around the city.

B. In yesterday's _____, the newspaper said we shouldn't have fireworks this year.

C. The special sale helped improve the store's _____

D. The _____ story about fashions showed how to paint T-shirts.

E. I read the _____ of the movie and decided not to see it.

F. The newspaper's _____ grew because many people liked its stories on local sports.

G. Flutes and horns are shaped like _____.

H. Lee works at the local newspaper, running the _____ press.

Newspapers

1. Use the chart to help you remember what you read. For each topic, write the section of the newspaper where the story would probably be found.

Topic	Newspaper Section
A. a state law that would change the voting age	
B. a World Series baseball game	
C. an election in France	
D. the paper's opinion on pollution in the city	
E. new rules for the parks in a city	
F. a speech given by the country's president	
G. an expert's opinions on taxes	

2. Why do you think newspapers have many sections?

_____

_____

_____

_____

3. Choose two sections of a newspaper that interest you. How might you read the stories in those sections differently?

_____

_____

_____

_____

4. Suppose your job was to sell ads for your school or local newspaper. How would you get people to buy an ad?

_____

_____

_____

_____

Acknowledgments

Photo Credits

Cover photos: (top) BananaStock/Punchstock; (bottom, L-R) Stockbyte Silver/Getty Images; Comstock Images/Punchstock; Digital Vision/Punchstock; Dave Bartruff/Digital Vision/Getty Images; **Page:** 8 Rob Nelnychuk/Brand X Pictures/Jupiter Images; 10 Jenny Mills/Photo Library.com; 12 © Dennis MacDonald/PhotoEdit; 14 © Steve Skjold/Skjold Photographs; 22 © Paul Souders/DanitaDelimont.com; 24 Ron Dahlquist/Stone/Getty Images; 26 Brand X Pictures; 28 NASA Marshall Space Flight Center (NASA-MSFC); 36 © Tony Freeman/PhotoEdit; 38 © W. Geiersperger/Corbis; 40, 42, 108 © David Young-Wolff/PhotoEdit; 50 The Art Archive/Ragab Papyrus Institute, Cairo/Dagli Orti; 52 AP Images; 54 © Kirk Condyles/The Image Works; 56, 134, 136 Getty Images; 64 EclectiCollections™; 66 Schalkwijk/Art Resource, NY; 68 Courtesy of the Library of Congress; 70 Panapress/Getty Images, Inc.; 78 The Kobal Collection/Chaplin/United Artists; 80 Miramax/The Kobal Collection; 82 Amblin/Universal/The Kobal Collection; 84 AP Images; 92, 96, 126 © Bettmann/Corbis. All Rights Reserved.; 94, 122 The Granger Collection, New York; 98 © Jeff Greenberg/PhotoEdit; 106 PhotoDisc, Inc./Getty Images; 110 © Michelle D. Bridwell/PhotoEdit; 112 © Ted Streshinsky/Corbis; 120 "Returning from the Cotton Fields in South Carolina," ca. 1860, stereograph by Barbard, negative number 47843. © Collection of The New York Historical Society; 124 National Archives and Records Administration; 138 Anglo-Enterprise/Vineyard/The Kobal Collection; 140 Getty Images; 148 George Bernard/Photo Researchers, Inc.; 150 © Susan Van Etten/PhotoEdit; 152 Renee/Photo Researchers, Inc.; 154 Amos Morgan/Photodisc Green/Getty Images; 162 ImageState/International Stock; 164 Will Hart; 166 Will Faller; 168 Pearson Education/Prentice Hall College

Text Credits

• "Rock Around the Clock" recorded by Bill Haley & His Comets, Decca Records, 1954. "(We're Gonna) Rock Around the Clock" written by Max C. Freedman and James E. Myers. © 1981 Myers Music, Inc.
• *Don Juan.* 1926. Dir. Alan Crosland. © Turner Entertainment Company. All Rights Reserved.
• *Saturday Night Fever* (music). Copyright © RSO Records, 1977.
• *Saturday Night Fever* (movie). TM & Copyright © 1977 Paramount Pictures. All rights reserved.
• *Star Wars: I—The Phantom Menace*, written and directed by George Lucas. © 2001 Lucasfilm Ltd. and TM. All Rights Reserved.
• *Star Wars: II—Attack of the Clones.* Dir. George Lucas. © 2002 Lucasfilm Ltd. and TM. All Rights Reserved.
• *Star Wars: Episode III—Revenge of the Sith*, written and directed by George Lucas. © 2005 Lucasfilm Ltd. and TM. All Rights Reserved. Used under authorization. "STAR WARS" and all associated characters, logos and other elements are the property of Lucasfilm Ltd.
• *Star Wars: IV—A New Hope*, written and directed by George Lucas. TM and © 1977, 1997, 2004 Lucasfilm Ltd. All Rights Reserved.
• *Star Wars: V—The Empire Strikes Back.* Dir. Irvin Kershner. TM and © 1980, 1997, 2004 Lucasfilm Ltd. All Rights Reserved.

• *Star Wars: VI—Return of the Jedi.* Dir. Richard Marquand. TM and © 1983, 1997, 2004 Lucasfilm Ltd. All Rights Reserved.
• *E.T.* 1982. Dir. Steven Spielberg. TM & © 2001 Universal Studios.
• *Harry Potter and the Sorcerer's Stone* (movie). Dir. Chris Columbus. Harry Potter and the Sorcerer's Stone, Artwork and Photographs © 2001 Warner Bros. Other supplementary material, package artwork, design and summary © 2002 Warner Home Video, and AOL Time Warner Company, 4000 Warner Blvd., Burbank, CA 91522. Harry Potter Publishing Rights © J.K. Rowling. HARRY POTTER characters, names and related indicia are trademarks of and © Warner Bros.
• *Harry Potter and the Chamber of Secrets* (movie). Dir. Chris Columbus. Harry Potter and the Chamber of Secrets © 2002 MIRACLE Productions GmbH and Co. KG Artwork and Photographs © 2002 Warner Bros. Supplementary material, package artwork, design and summary © 2003 Warner Home Video, and AOL Time Warner Company, 4000 Warner Blvd., Burbank, CA 91522. Harry Potter Publishing Rights © J.K. Rowling. HARRY POTTER characters, names and related indicia are trademarks of and © Warner Bros.
• *Harry Potter and the Prisoner of Azkaban* (movie). Dir. Alfonso Cuaron. HARRY POTTER characters, names and related indicia are trademarks of and © Warner Bros. Entertainment Inc. Harry Potter Publishing Rights © J.K. Rowling. Harry Potter and the Prisoner of Azkaban © 2004 P of A Productions Limited. Package Design and Supplementary Material Compilation © 2004 Warner Bros. Entertainment Inc. Distributed by Warner Home Video Inc., 4000 Warner Blvd., Burbank, CA 91522. All Rights Reserved.
• *Jaws.* Dir. Steven Spielberg. © 1975 Universal Studios. All Rights Reserved. © 2000 Universal Studios. All Rights Reserved.
• *Jaws 2.* Dir. Jeannot Szwarc. © 1978 Universal Studios. All Rights Reserved. © 2001 Universal Studios. All Rights Reserved.
• *Frankenstein* by Mary Shelley. 1818. Copyright © 2003 by Barnes & Noble, Inc. All rights reserved.
• *Dandelion Wine* by Ray Bradbury. Copyright © 1946, 1947, 1950, 1951, 1952, 1953, 1954, 1955, 1957 by Ray Bradbury. Copyright © 1956, 1957 by The Curtis Publishing Company. All rights reserved. New York: Bantam Books. A Bantam/Spectra Book, published by arrangement with Doubleday.
• *Fahrenheit 451* (book) by Ray Bradbury. Copyright © 1953, 1981 by Ray Bradbury. All rights reserved. A Del Rey® Book published by The Random House Publishing Group. New York: Random House.
• *Fahrenheit 451* (movie). 1966. Dir. Francois Truffaut. © 1966 Vineyard Films, Ltd. All Rights Reserved. © 2003 Universal Studios. All Rights Reserved.

Staff Credits

Members of the AMP™ QReads™ team: Melania Benzinger, Karen Blonigen, Carol Bowling, Michelle Carlson, Kazuko Collins, Nancy Condon, Barbara Drewlo, Sue Gulsvig, Daren Hastings, Laura Henrichsen, Ruby Hogen-Chin, Julie Johnston, Mary Kaye Kuzma, Julie Maas, Daniel Milowski, Carrie O'Connor, Julie Theisen, Mary Verrill, Mike Vineski, Charmaine Whitman